"After you've read *Power Points For Success*, you'll be motivated to leave the ruts. The stories and lessons in this book are simple, yet profound. It's fantastic!"

— Robert H. Schuller
Pastor-Motivational Speaker

"Good reading, good principles, good examples. You will benefit from it."

— Zig Ziglar
Author-Motivational Speaker

"If you're ready to increase your love, thinking, happiness, friendships, and money, read this book NOW!"

— Mark Victor Hansen
Co-Author of *Chicken Soup for the Soul*

"This thought and action provoking book is bound to change the way you look at what you can do. Read it."

— Tom Hopkins
Sales Trainer

"Bob Harrison is one of my favorite teachers. He is dynamic and has powerful things to say. This book will impact your life. You will find yourself reading it over and over again."

— Peter Lowe
America's Premiere Success Co-Ordinator

"Bob Harrison has a way to pull out of each article truths that will energize and empower you."

— John Mason
Author of *An Enemy Called Average*

"Bob Harrison's principles of Biblical leadership have helped bring my life to a level of success greater than I had ever dreamed. This book will change your life too."

— Brian M. Gillespie
Vice-President Operations
ITT Sheraton Reservations

"Bob Harrison's teaching gives me more 'walk-away' than anyone's. You will find insights that will work for you now."

— Merrill Eichenberger
Television Info-mercial Producer

Power Points For Success

101 Electrifying Stories
From Today's Headlines
To Empower Your Dreams
and Brighten Your Day

by Bob Harrison

Honor Books
Tulsa, Oklahoma

Third Printing

Power Points For Success
ISBN 1-56292-125-8
Copyright © 1997 by Bob Harrison
P.O. Box 701890
Tulsa, Oklahoma 74170-9926

Published by Honor Books
P.O. Box 55388
Tulsa, Oklahoma 74155

All net profits from the first printing of this book are being donated to the Christian Leaders Charity Fund.

Acknowledgments

A picture of the late Norman Vincent Peale sits across from my writing table. Inscribed on the photograph are these words: "Dare to be what you want to be and *can* be."

I would like to thank all those friends and peers who have challenged and inspired me to increase my teaching arsenal by adding books to my best-selling tape seminar teaching tapes.

Special thanks go to some of my friends and mentors: Peter Lowe, America's Premiere Success Seminar Conductor, for his inspiration and encouragement; Zig Ziglar, for all of his input and motivation; Dexter Yager, Mark Victor Hansen, Dr. Patrick Quillin, Tim Flynn, Tom Hopkins, Robert Schuller, John Mason, and members of our Christian Leaders Organization, all of whom have encouraged and/or inspired me more than they will ever know.

Also, a special note of thanks must go to my copyeditor, Jimmy Peacock, and to my executive assistants, Michelle Montes and Jodi Cook, secretaries Tiffany Demuth and Crystol Harrison, and marketing manager Chris Ophus, for their hours and hours of dedicated work.

In addition, I want to express my great appreciation to Keith Provance, Dave Bordon, John Roe, Cristine Bolley, and the staff of Honor Books who have been absolutely tremendous to work with.

In particular my appreciation goes to my wife of 30-plus years, Cindy, without whose love, assistance, and commitment to excellence none of this would have been possible, and my eight children (five by birth and three by marriage), all of whom have been a blessing and inspiration beyond measure.

Last, I want to thank my mom and dad, who provided me with godly examples of a loving, stable home and a spiritual foundation that positively impact every day of my life.

Table of Contents

Preface

The valuable book described in the above headline is the one you hold in your hand! Within 30 days your life could totally change as a result of learning and applying the success strategies contained in it.

Years ago, when I was drowning in a sea of multi-million-dollar debt, exhausted from grabbing for "success straws," I would have given almost anything to have the knowledge and wisdom contained between the covers of this book.

Instead, I had to begin a desperate search for answers — real answers — that could provide me a needed "lifeline to personal and financial victory."

One weekend while speaking in Michigan, I met a millionaire industrialist who reintroduced me to a book that he said "had the greatest 'success secrets' ever written." To my amazement, I discovered

"Power — the basic energy needed to initiate and sustain action."
— Bob Harrison

that he was talking about the Bible. I had always thought of the Bible solely as a book of theology. Now a successful businessman was telling me that it was also a handbook of successful financial principles and victorious living keys.

Over the next several months, I intensely studied it to discover its living and financial victory secrets. I also began an intensive program of tape listening and reading.

By combining my newly acquired Biblical knowledge with my business acumen, I soon began to experience a total turnaround in every area of my life.

Financially, over one-half of my multi-million-dollar debt was eliminated in one day. I began to experience a supernatural increase in investments, real estate deals, and personal finances. I had become an overcomer.

Personally, I became much more positive. My values and priorities changed as fresh love rose up from within for my wife and children.

Spiritually, I experienced a complete renewal as my life took on a new vibrancy and meaning.

Over the next few years, I devoured hundreds of additional books, collected and computerized thousands of quotes, and interviewed scores of leaders and achievers from all walks of life to learn their success secrets.

Soon, business organizations, marketing groups, and churches began to book me to share my valuable knowledge. As people applied these strategies, many of them began to experience dramatic changes in their personal lives and businesses such as evidenced by the following testimonials.

A businessman in Oklahoma wrote: "Now a few months later, signs and miracles abound in my life. My business has more than doubled since the middle of the year. I have gotten very involved in my church. My marriage has never been happier; my wife and I are acting like two teenagers in love. I've been totally cured of cancer, and I've lost 75 pounds."

From California came a call from a pastor who told me later that the day after I shared with his congregation on increase, more than 36 members of his church had 24-hour breakthroughs!

An Amway Double Diamond Distributor called me and said excitedly: "This teaching has changed my life."

And a businessman in Washington testified: "In the last year my income has gone from $25,000 a year to $140,000."

Plus, there are scores and scores of others too numerous to list.

Because of the dramatic changes taking place in people's lives, the speaking arena door flew wide open for me. I have traveled to all 50 states, been to nearly 50 countries, spoken to audiences of 20,000 and more, taught at $5,000-per-person seminars, shared the stage with the world's most famous people, and appeared numerous times on radio talk shows and national television — *all because these keys work!*

You will notice that each of the "power points" in the book is introduced via a newspaper headline and/or unusual story. This was done to provide a memory recall mechanism and in many cases to show humorous or practical applications of the principles.

Also, many of the different "power points" introduced in this book center around interesting and/or humorous incidents in my life or the lives of famous achievers. From the stories, you will learn how these strategies were activated for success.

At the conclusion of each article you are asked to make your own headline. Let your imagination soar as you answer the questions posed to jog your thinking and release creativity.

As a further assistance, a verse of Scripture is quoted to provide the Biblical foundation for the success principle set forth.

If you are like most people, you are wondering about the book title *Power Points*. I define "power" as the basic energy needed to initiate and sustain action, enabling one to translate intention into reality. It is a quality without which people cannot change and leaders cannot lead. A "point" is defined as an exact spot or location.

This book you hold can be your personal "power point." By activating these strategies, plans, and actions, you can enjoy maximum achievement, fresh romance, spiritual renewal, and/or enduring fulfillment.

Why settle for survival when you can live a life of power and significance? Be all that you desire to be and all that God created you to be. Think of what you have to look forward to.

MAKE YOUR OWN HEADLINE

What is the best — and quickest — way that you can activate the "power points" of this book into your life?

...he...giveth strength and power unto his people....
Psalm 68:35

Turtle Falls From Sky Hits Man In Car Sends Him To Hospital

Police report that a Fort Lauderdale man was leisurely driving down the street in his convertible with the top down enjoying the fresh air and sunshine. Suddenly something crashed on his head. According to emergency room doctors, the object that hit him was an airborne turtle.

Officers on the scene surmised that a sea gull had apparently snatched a turtle from the ground, begun its flight, found that the turtle was too heavy to hold onto, lost its grip, and dropped the turtle, causing the accident.

The problem this bird encountered is a problem achievers oftentimes encounter. They are so good at doing so many things that they attempt to do too much. Oftentimes the weight of it all becomes more than they can handle, and they lose their grip on their time, their health, and their priorities.

Radio commentator James Dobson says that he believes that overcommitment is currently the number one destroyer of marriages.[1]

Not long ago Time magazine did a feature on stress and overcommitment. In the article, Dr. Joel Elkes of the University of Louisville exclaimed: "Our mode of life itself, the way we live, is emerging as today's principal cause of illness."[2]

Several years ago Denis Waitley found himself in a state of overcommitment "with an overloaded calendar but not really building any lasting success."

"Take spare
moments to
quietly
meditate or
clear your
mind."
— Ruth Stapleton
Peale

"I had everything going for me...and nothing coming together. I had a house but not the home life. I had the family...but not the spiritual foundation so vital to relationship."[3]

If you feel under stress and overcommitted, then read on.

RUTH STAPLETON PEALE

Ms. Peale, the widow of Norman Vincent Peale, is an author and lecturer. She and I shared the stage together at a success seminar in Little Rock, Arkansas. The following are some keys I have learned from her to help reduce the weight of life while continuing to fly high.

GET-A-GRIP KEYS

1. KNOW YOUR PRIORITIES: Constantly remind yourself what your personal priorities are. Make a list of what is really important to you in the long run.

2. TAKE THINGS AS THEY COME: Life is filled with moments that give rise to tension. Retrain your brain not to worry about the unknown. React to things as they come, and you will be able to solve problems that arise.

3. MAKE TIME FOR RELAXATION: Don't just think of relaxation in terms of weekends, holidays, and vacations. Each day carve out little niches of relaxation time to reduce the pressure, clear your mind, and become empowered.

4. BRING GOD INTO YOUR SITUATIONS: If you seek His guidance and receive His blessing of peace, you will be better able to handle any situation. Take time for meditation and prayer.

Don't let the extra weights of tension, overcommitment, and misplaced priorities cause you to lose your grip on what is really important in your life. In trying to hold onto and/or do too much, you could risk losing it all.

What can you do to reduce the cares of life and increase personal calmness today? Have you clearly defined what is and is not important to you?

"For my yoke is easy...my burden is light."
Matthew 11:30

A Monkey On Their Backs

Sixteen thousand wild monkeys are imported into the United States each year from the tropical regions of the earth. To prevent the spread of infectious diseases, these monkeys must be cared for at a quarantine facility for a month before they are shipped anywhere in the States.

Dr. Kenneth Blanchard

"You are helping your people too much if you take responsibility for the care and feeding of their monkeys," says Dr. Kenneth Blanchard, co-author of the *One-Minute Manager*.

"Monkeys" in this context refers to the tasks, jobs, or problems that are the responsibility of other people, normally subordinates, friends, or children.

You put a monkey on your back when you desire to help someone and find yourself saying, "Let me help," or even worse, "Let me do it for you." That person walks away thirty pounds lighter, because now the monkey (the problem) is yours.

If you put too many of other people's monkeys on your back it will add stress to your life and reduce the time available for your main responsibilities. It will also create role-reversal, because then your subordinates and friends will be checking up on how you are doing with the problem.

Dr. Blanchard suggests three responses for keeping the monkeys on other people's backs and off of yours.

THREE RESPONSES TO KEEP THE MONKEYS OFF YOUR BACK

1. SUPPORTIVE RESPONSE: State that you understand the complexity of the other's problem and that you are willing to talk with them about how they (not you) can get it solved.

2. DELEGATING RESPONSE: Inform others that this is their responsibility, but give them some suggestions they might try.

3. COACHING RESPONSE: If you feel others do not have the ability to handle their monkeys, then give them specific directions. Explain the next move, or strategy, that you would recommend, and then supervise what they do.

Blanchard teaches that the two biggest problems in possessing other people's monkeys are: they must be cared for and fed by you, and their former owners now check to see how you are doing with their monkeys.

MAKE YOUR OWN HEADLINE

Are other people's monkeys (problems) "driving you bananas?" How can you determine which ones need to be cared for, returned, or disposed of?

And Moses' father-in-law said to him, "The thing that you are doing is not good. You will surely wear out,...you cannot do it alone."
Exodus 18:17,18 NASB

Airliner Loses Door In Flight

Passengers saved a flight attendant from being sucked out of a plane when its door flew open three minutes after takeoff from Chicago. Safety investigators are trying to determine why the metal door on the aircraft opened in flight. The loud swishing noise and suction force caused panic among the passengers.

The purpose of doors is to provide entrance and exit. However, if they open at the wrong time — as happened above — they can cause real problems. This is true on airliners, in bedrooms, and at the office.

Let me illustrate with an experience that happened to me with my friend Dick Withnell.

Several years ago I was visiting with Dick at his successful automobile dealership in the Northwest. During the course of our conversation he mentioned to me that his business sales volume and income had greatly increased over the last few years. However, even though he was excited about the situation he actually was feeling greater stress and having a more difficult time focusing on important tasks. He asked me for suggestions.

Over the next hour I analyzed the "flow" of his schedule. I soon came to realize that one of his main problems was the door to his office. He had no control over when it would open or close. Employees and customers would enter and leave through the door at will.

Power Point

"Lost time can never be found again."
— Benjamin Franklin

Although it is admirable to be accessible, this "open door policy" was causing him to have no control over interruptions and distractions. It was also robbing him of the privacy that is necessary for creative thinking, long-term planning, and meaningful conversations.

When the dealership was smaller this "open door policy" was not a problem. Now sometimes his office seemed as busy as Grand Central Station during rush hour. I advised him to remain "touchable" but to take control of interruptions. I also assured him that no one should be offended by this action.

He activated my recommendation by moving his secretary's office next to his and giving her the open door. He still remained accessible but now she answered the phone and served as the "gatekeeper" to his door. His productivity went back up and his stress level went down.

A common characteristic of most achievers is their appreciation of the value of time and their understanding of their need to be in control of it.

Victor Hugo once said, "He who every morning plans the transactions of the day and follows out that plan, carries a thread that will guide him through the labyrinth of the most busy life."

If you want to be truly successful and effective, you must maintain mastery of your time and your interruptions in particular. They can be one of the biggest problems you face in managing time.

The secret is to adopt a "screen-door policy" rather than an "open-door policy." Have someone screen your calls and guests.

If you do not control when your doors open, the "loud swishing noise" you hear may be the sound of productivity being sucked out of your life.

Who is in control of your "doors," you or others? Is your work routine proactive or responsive?

And no one could come into the inner court...except with the king's permission...or they would be put to death.
Esther 4:11 (author's paraphrase)

Giant Sinkhole Swallows Home

The gaping mouth of a giant sinkhole sucked down a million-dollar home in a prestigious San Francisco neighborhood. The sinkhole, so big that a ten-story building could fit inside, was apparently created when water runoff from several days of torrential rains collapsed a century-old sewer line and washed away the earth beneath the home's foundation. Engineers believe that they can save the adjacent three-story luxury residence by firming up its foundation.

Many homes are falling into giant sinkholes, and not just in San Francisco. All across America homes are collapsing in the relationship arena as marriages and families are suddenly sucked into the sinkhole of separation and divorce.

Like the million-dollar homes in California, these marriages appear to be beautiful and stately. Then suddenly, one day everything collapses. This is because underneath, in the land of the invisible, the very foundation of the relationship has washed away over time.

What causes these washouts?

Several factors can cause marital washout. Often, it is a result of a lifestyle of continuous stress, which attacks a couple's intimacy and communication. Other times it may be wrong priorities brought on by an overfocus on self.

For many achievers, the cause of marital washout is the boredom that sets in when old dreams and goals are attained and new ones are not created.

"Stability is an absolute necessity for a successful marriage."
— Gary Smalley

Here's how you can avoid having your marriage relationship crumble into a giant sinkhole by firming up its foundation.

MARRIAGE FOUNDATION BUILDERS

1. ROMANCE: Schedule quiet times alone together. Never stop dating. Practice being tender and caring to one another.

2. PLAY: Laugh, have fun, and enjoy life. Schedule recreational activities that both of you enjoy.

3. ESCAPE: Take trips together to dream spots. Periodically break your normal schedules and routine of life.

4. PRAISE: Nourish each other's ego and self-image through positive affirmations and praise.

5. AWARENESS: Become more aware of each other's needs, desires, and yearnings.

6. COMMUNICATION: Learn to listen carefully to each other as you express your deepest feelings.

7. WORSHIP: Share common spiritual experiences together. This will add depth, power, and intimacy to your relationship.

Add your own foundation builders to this list. You will not only avoid giant sinkholes, but you will enjoy a more exciting and loving relationship.

MAKE YOUR OWN HEADLINE

What are you doing to add depth to your marriage foundation as you build height to your career? What can you do to add significance and security to your relationship?

The wise person builds his home upon a firm foundation, and when the storms come, it falls not.
Matthew 7:24,25 (author's paraphrase)

ROBERT SCHULLER

Have you ever felt like your life was upside down and that you were plummeting toward personal or financial destruction?

Dr. Schuller started a church in California several years ago because he was convinced he had a powerful message to share with people who were struggling with adversity in life, those who had no religion and never went to church. He wanted to help them by sharing faith or relationship with Christ with those who had never experienced living this way.

This underlying belief has guided him because he believed that if he could take his strength and energy and expend it in one place, then certainly after a lifetime he ought to be able to have a great church and leave something for the world.

Robert Schuller is known not only as a great pastor and orator, but also as a "Possibility Thinker." He says that this happened one day when he was

"The word 'possibility' penetrates into the subconscious mind and calls forth powers to 'Turn On.'"
— Robert Schuller

reading his Bible and the words of Jesus entered his mind: "Nothing will be impossible for you."

Possibility Thinking is simply "focusing faith on achieving definite goals."

THE POSSIBILITY THINKER'S CREED

When faced with a mountain,
I WILL NOT QUIT!
I will keep on striving
until
I climb over,
find a pass through,
tunnel underneath,
or
simply stay
and
turn the mountain
into a gold mine
with
God's help!

MAKE YOUR OWN HEADLINE

What are you doing to activate Possibility Thinking Power in your life? How can you become a bigger thinker?

...Nothing will be impossible for you.
Matthew 17:20 NIV

C ash flow, profits, and recognition are increased whenever a drawing card is discovered. This is true with operas, businesses, sports events as well as in personal life.

THE SECRET WEAPON OF RAPPORT

You can become empowered with a "drawing card" that will bring favor and financial increase into your life. It is called "rapport."

I define "rapport" as an invisible bond between people.

Sales trainer Tony Robbins says, "Rapport is the ultimate tool for producing results with people. It is the ability to enter someone else's world and cause them to feel that you understand and care for them."[1]

Rapport is created by discovering things in common. The two most effective methods used to create rapport are: "mirroring" — looking, acting and/or talking like the other party — and "establishing commonality" — finding or creating common areas of interest.

When properly used, these methods can cause you to...

BE TREATED LIKE A VIP EVERY TIME

Several years ago my wife and I attended a VIP reception preceding the Washington National Charity Banquet. Pat Robertson, former presidential candidate and current head of the Christian Broadcasting Network, was one of the designated celebrities and was being mobbed by well-wishers.

I desired to personally meet him and maybe begin a relationship. I knew that by the evening's end most of those who had greeted him would be nothing more than a happy blur in his memory. How could I stand out and in some way create a memorable occasion with him?

Since I understood how rapport is created, I knew that somehow I had to use "commonality" to create a bond, a mutual point of interest.

Having learned earlier that the zip code I live in represented the second largest contribution base for his failed presidential bid, I went into action.

I boldly walked up to him, shook his hand, and stated, "Hi Pat, my name is Bob Harrison, and I live in zip code 74136."

He paused, look confused, and contemplated my words. Then it hit him what I was referring to. He grabbed me and burst into wild laughter. We had a good conversation and have been together several times since.

I went from an unknown to a VIP — at a VIP function — when I found and expressed a common interest.

Studies of successful people have shown that most of them possess a great talent for creative rapport. If you will perfect these techniques, you will release an invisible "phantom force" that will cause people to remember you and want to be around you.

When you meet new people, do you think in terms of entering into their world? How can you form or strengthen bonds with family members, friends, and business associates by better using rapport?

Wash and perfume yourself and put on your best clothes....
Ruth 3:3 NIV

Rich, But Sad and Lonely

She makes millions of dollars per year and is known worldwide as a television media celebrity. Now a shocking report reveals that, "...she is sad, full of regrets, and lonely."

Money and fame cannot keep an individual from feeling lonely. That feeling of isolation and detachment can strike even in the middle of a crowd.

A feeling of loneliness not only affects a person's attitude, relationships, and outlook on life, it can also affect his physical health. The National Institute of Health reports, "The most predictive risk factor for heart disease is loneliness" which is nothing more than a deficiency of love.[1]

CATHERINE MARSHALL

Unlike the television celebrity featured in the headline above, her loneliness did not come from a life of misplaced priorities. It came as a result of her husband's death. She states, "For a time during busy hours one can forget the pain of loneliness. Then some tiny thing, anything, brings it flooding back."[2]

Loneliness might also come as a result of temporary separation, as evidenced by a letter she received from her young son who went to camp for the first time. He wrote, "I am very homesick. Could you come and take me home before Sunday? I would like it very much. If you can't, would you please come and take me home Monday?"[3]

If you are feeling detached, sad, or lonely, here are some secrets that I have discovered that will help.

SEVEN SURE-FIRE WAYS TO BEAT LONELINESS

1. CONTACT OTHERS: Make a list of everyone you know: loved ones, friends, and acquaintances. Make it a point to contact them regularly.

2. GET INVOLVED: No matter where you live or what your interests or skills may be, there are people who need your help. Show interest in their lives. It will bring joy to yours.

3. DEVELOP NEW DREAMS: Dreams give hope and spark to life. Find new things to achieve. An elderly triathlon runner once said, "No one is ever alone who has a dream."

4. EAT PROPERLY: Low blood sugar or improper diet can magnify negative feelings. Check your food intake.

5. REST: Recharge your body. Tired people tend to lean toward their problems and respond negatively to situations.

6. COUNT RIGHT: Focus on the good things that have happened and are happening in your life.

7. REMEMBER GOD: You are never really alone because God loves you, and He is as near as your prayers.

MAKE YOUR OWN HEADLINE

Which of the above strategies can you implement to drive loneliness out of your life?

_____

...the God of love and peace will be with you.
2 Corinthians 13:11 NIV
_____

ZIG ZIGLAR

America's Premiere Success Teacher is an incredible man. Three times he has been cited in the *Congressional Record*, "For contributions made to elevating sales as a profession." Yet he is down to earth, likable, real, and touchable.

Sharing the stage with him is an exciting experience. We have been together numerous times, from Hartford to Honolulu and from Green Bay to El Paso.

Zig is best known as a sales and motivational speaker.

However, he believes so strongly that a relationship with Jesus Christ is a necessary foundation to success that he could almost be classified as a "minister in disguise."

Here are some of his success nuggets that I have collected from our times together:

ZIG ZIGLAR POWER POINTS

"No individual can rise above the pictures that have been painted in his mind."

"Change where you are by changing what goes into your mind."

"If you do the things you ought to do when you ought to do them, the day will come when you can do the things you want to do when you want to do them."

"Regardless of your past, tomorrow is a clean slate."

"You can have everything you want in life if you help enough people get what they want."

"You were designed for accomplishment, engineered for success, and endowed with Seeds of Greatness."

"The greatest enemy of excellence is good."

"When you are tough on yourself, life is easier on you."

And my favorite...

"If you don't like the output, then change the input."

> ### Power Point
>
> "If you don't like the output, then change the input."
> — Zig Ziglar

MAKE YOUR OWN HEADLINE

How are you actively pursuing the wisdom of others? What input can you add to your life that will elevate the output of your dreams?

A wise man will hear, and will increase learning; and a man of understanding shall attain unto wise counsels.
Proverbs 1:5

Heart Attacks Reduced By Up To 75%

Doctors are astonished by a British medical study that concludes a dime's worth of vitamin E, taken daily, can reduce heart attacks by up to 75 percent.

DR. PATRICK QUILLIN

Millions of people may suffer unnecessarily with poor health and die prematurely because they are not taking ten cents worth of nutrients and are not following the basic principles of health taught throughout the Bible.

My friend, Dr. Quillin, who is one of America's foremost nutritionists, lecturers, and broadcasters, says that the problem is that "after years of neglect, bodies that are built for activity become bodies that can barely get off the couch. Then, when these starving and poorly maintained bodies begin to break down, potent drugs are oftentimes used to mask the symptoms of the illnesses, rather than deal with the underlying cause of the disease, which oftentimes is improper diet and/or lack of exercise."[1]

Dr. Quillin states, "You cannot enjoy life as God intended nor accomplish your 'mission' if your body wears out too soon." He believes that people's lives will change when they come to the realization that "God's purpose for providing food is to nourish the body with essential nutrients found in plants and animals and to provide a physical connection with the invisible God Who provides it."[2]

From his book H*ealing Secrets From the Bible*, here are some keys to better health.

DR. QULLIN'S ABC'S OF BETTER HEALTH

A. ANTIOXIDANTS: Curtail aging and prevent disease by eating plenty of fresh whole fruits and vegetables.

B. BACK MAINTENANCE: The spinal cord is an extension of the brain. Keep it aligned and strong.

C. CHEW FOOD THOROUGHLY: When food is swallowed too quickly it cannot be absorbed into the body.

D. DRINK FLUIDS BETWEEN MEALS: Drink minimal amounts of fluids while you are eating. They dilute digestive juices. Drink water between meals.

E. TAKE VITAMIN E: Studies have shown that the greatest nutritional risk factor for heart disease is a long-term deficiency of vitamin E.[3]

MAKE YOUR OWN HEADLINE

When and what has it cost you to be sick? Describe what you are doing nutritionally to improve your health.

Eat what is good and delight yourself with rich nourishment.
Isaiah 55:2 (author's paraphrase)

New York Cabbie Sick After Being Taken For A 1500-Mile Ride

Police report that a cabbie drove a man all the way from New York to Michigan and back, and then got a bad check for the $2,000 fare. Three days after the 32-hour trip the cabbie was still sick in bed.

One big question came to my mind as I read the above article: why would anyone be so foolish as to invest so much time, energy, and expense into a job or customer without being assured of payment?

Then I realized this is what many achievers and businesses do regularly. They provide goods and/or services to customers based solely on a purchase order number, a verbal order, or a customer's promise to pay.

I could not begin to count the scores of prayer requests and counseling calls that I have received over the years from people who were having financial difficulties because of slow-paying or uncollectible accounts. In most instances, having a simple credit policy would have eliminated their problems.

LOSS PREVENTION STRATEGIES

1. REDUCE EXPOSURE: On large projects or orders demand payment as the job progresses (such as one-third at inception, one-third at midpoint,

and one-third at completion). Having such a policy can reduce your financial exposure by 67 to 90 percent.

2. ELIMINATE ACCOUNTS RECEIVABLE: When possible eliminate the risks altogether by accepting credit cards, subscribing to a check guarantee system, offering bank financing, or just saying, "Cash only."

3. ESATBLISH CUSTOMER CREDIT LIMITS: If you must extend credit, have predetermined policies of how much credit you are willing to extend based upon a customer's credit history or collateral.

4. INSPECT ACCOUNTS REGULARLY: Have a system of regular follow-up and contact with accounts.

5. PRAY ABOUT YOUR ACCOUNTS RECEIVABLE: Throughout the Bible it is revealed that the Holy Spirit can give understanding, wisdom, warning, and favor.

The secret is to remember that it is not what you bill, but rather what you actually collect that is important. Instituting the above policies will allow you to spend your time *making money*, not collecting it.

MAKE YOUR OWN HEADLINE

What can you do to actually collect more of what you earn? How can you better avoid collection problems?

Be thou diligent to know the state of thy flocks, and look well to thy herds.
Proverbs 27:23

When Capt. Scott O'Grady hauled himself to his feet after ejecting from his flaming F-16 in northern Bosnia's wooded hills, he knew exactly what to do next. He was bruised and dazed, but the training he had received at Survival and Escape School had prepared him for the crisis.

Because of his training, Scott O'Grady passed the ultimate test. He was able to survive five and a half days of hiding by living on rainwater, wild plants, and bugs.

The key to the training he received at the survival school he attended is that his instructors did not teach just survival skills, but also a survival attitude.

What is a "survival attitude?" It is a force on the inside of a person that enables him to rise up, bounce back, and even shine in the face of negative circumstances. This is not something a person is born with. It is a learned behavior.

A prime example of another person who developed this vital skill is...

DEXTER YAGER

Dexter Yager and his charming wife Birdie operate what is probably the largest network marketing organization in the world. My wife and I have been privileged to speak with them on several occasions. He likes to share how he developed the survival attitude as a child.

THE SURVIVAL ATTITUDE

"While in the sixth grade, I got the idea of buying soda pop for five cents a bottle, and then turning around and selling it for a dime to construction people working in the area. There were no vending machines nearby and the workers couldn't take off work to visit the stores. I used the ice from my mother's refrigerator. Immediately, my business was a great success. I started selling cases and cases of pop. Soon I was earning more than many adults.

"Some businessmen learned of my success and came in with their own ice and drinks. They were much bigger than me. If I wanted to keep my business I had to fight. That's what I did. I hired some kids to help and worked harder. We offered more drinks for the price. We had a better selection. And on hot days we made sure we never ran out of ice!

"We won the war. Our competition ran away. For them it was just another business, but to me it was a dream come true."[2]

If you desire to be a high achiever, you must learn how to struggle against the obstacles that get in your way. A survival attitude is a learned behavior. It is developed every time you resist the urge to quit and instead fight back. Each action helps to form a habit, and habits create your character and your destiny.

MAKE YOUR OWN HEADLINE

What steps can you take to form the habit of resisting adversity? How can you increase your survival attitude?

[I pray that you will be] strengthened with all power, according to His [God's] glorious might, for the attaining of all steadfastness and patience....
Colossians 1:11 NASB

Body Discovered Floating In Lake

Police are investigating the death of a man whose body was found floating near the shoreline.

Several years ago I was floating on the lake — the lake of life. I felt unmotivated, directionless, emotionally drained, and literally "dead in the water."

I arrived in this condition because of a series of events that had taken place in my life. I had sold my Chrysler dealership, disengaged myself from the automobile leasing business, and moved the family from California to Tulsa. I felt strongly that I was to make major changes in my life, but I had not yet "caught" the vision — and calling — of what I was to do next.

Not having a future to focus on, I found myself continually looking back. I was making money, but I felt that I was going nowhere.

All of this began to change in one day when my wife presented me with a special poem she had written for my fortieth birthday.

As I read and meditated upon her inspired verse, something astonishing began to happen to me. The words — and the spirit behind them —

reached down and grabbed me out of my "quicksand of directionless." They sparked hope and vitality back into my life.

Her inspiring poem caused me to realize that all my acquired business acumen and past financial victories and struggles — combined with my biblical knowledge and anointing — were to be used to help others live overcoming, victorious lives. It was as if God was using her words to command my future to "come forth out of my past." This is a portion of what she wrote to me that fateful day.

To My Husband

Forty years have come and gone,
But the man inside has just been born.
Look out world, he's on the scene,
A man with vigor with a mind that's keen.

Forty years he's been growing tall,
But look out world, 'cause that ain't all.
This man's made of the super stuff,
That makes a man more than just tough.

A man prepared for life to succeed,
With vision and a call on him to heed.
A victor is he...a conqueror, yes,
He's no ordinary man...he's the best!

As a result of this "image-changing" verse, soon I was dreaming, preparing, writing, speaking about my life's assignment to this generation — achieving a life of increase and helping others!

Looking back on that event has caused me on many occasions to be a personal instrument of praise and encouragement to others who are in need of a "bounce back."

Jesus came to earth to bless, to heal, to bring encouragement and life to others. We are commanded to do the same.

MAKE YOUR OWN HEADLINE

How can you be a greater blessing and encouragement to others? Who has blessed you recently? Have you thanked them?

"...ye shall be a blessing...."
Zechariah 8:13

Nowadays even memorials must display images that are "politically correct." Therefore, controversial items, however factual, are often deliberately omitted.

For example, Eleanor Roosevelt's statue will not show her wearing her familiar fur wrap, FDR's ever-present cigarette holder will not be in evidence, and nowhere in the memorial will be displayed the wheelchair he used for the last 24 years of his life.

My friend Ken Kerr, who was Walt Disney's creative project director for the construction of the Epcot Center in Florida, teaches that "up to 70 percent of people make buying decisions based primarily upon the visual."[1]

Joe Girard, who for several years was the world's number one retail car salesman, says, "If the exterior image causes others to worry or be concerned about us or what we are, we can say goodbye to the sale."[2]

HARVEY MACKAY

He is a best-selling author and shares this same theme in his book, *Beware the Naked Man Who Offers You His Shirt.*

WRONG APPEARANCE CAN CAUSE YOUR DISAPPEARANCE

"Appearance...
is always what
sets you apart
from the
flock."
— Harvey
Mackay

"Next to quality, appearance is the single most important factor in selling products. Sometimes it's even more important. No one wants to hire people who wear raggedy, stained, down-at-the-heels clothes. You can always look like a winner if you want to, and so can everyone on your staff.

"Appearance, whether it comes through your advertising, your letterhead, or your clothes, is always what sets you apart from the flock."[3]

According to Dr. Edwin Louis Cole, author of *Maximized Manhood*, "The most powerful thing that can be done in life is to create an image."[4]

A Biblical example of the importance of a positive image can be found in the story of Joseph from the book of Genesis.

Pharaoh had a dream and desperately wanted the interpretation, which he was told could be provided by a man named Joseph who was then being held in his prison. Pharaoh commanded that Joseph be immediately brought to him. In spite of the urgency, before the guards would bring Joseph before the ruler he had to shave and change his clothes. Why? Because he had to have the right image.

MAKE YOUR OWN HEADLINE

Does your image and that of your business and your products reflect quality and success? Since you never get a second chance at a first impression, what can you do to improve that image?

When he [Joseph] had shaved and changed his clothes, he came
before Pharaoh.
Genesis 41:14

Dead Woman Sheds A Tear

Stunned doctors brought a dead woman back to life after seeing a tear roll down her cheek. The tear inspired the medical team to keep battling to save the woman, whose vital signs had ceased. Afterwards she said, "God has given me a second chance."

CINDY HARRISON

"The marriage between Bob and me died on May 26, 1972. I ran into my bedroom, fell down on the floor, and with tears streaming down my face, screamed out, 'GOD WHAT DO I DO? I DON'T LOVE HIM ANYMORE.'

"I was desperate. My negative feelings toward my husband had grown until I could hardly stand to be around him.

"Our crisis was not caused by any one big thing. Bob Harrison had always been faithful and provided well for the family. However, he had developed a negative attitude, was always criticizing me and others, and had gotten so busy that the kids and I were not getting needed attention.

"Because of this negative environment, without either of us fully realizing what was happening, love flew out of our home like a bird from a cage.

"I was not looking for a way out of the marriage. However, I just felt that I couldn't take it anymore.

"We would never have had a second chance at love except for my tearful decision to resurrect dead love...."
— Cindy Harrison

"At that moment God spoke to me from within and said, 'I can resurrect the love you once had for your husband.'

"Then a Bible verse came to my remembrance. It was Philippians 4:8, '...whatsoever things are of good report...if there be any praise, think on these things.'

"I came to realize what the root of our problems was. It was not just Bob's actions and seemingly uncaring attitude, but my negative response to him that was causing me to dwell on his shortcomings and faults.

MY HUSBAND'S GOOD REPORT LIST

"Pulling out a piece of paper, I began to activate the two words 'good report' from that verse into my life. I wrote down 'My Husband's Good Report List.' I listed the things I liked about him — the things he was doing right.

"Every morning and every night I read, confessed, and added to that list. I began to see more good things about him and our marriage. Gradually I found my attitude beginning to change. Soon thereafter my feelings and emotions responded as well.

"Now I understand what was happening. As I forced myself to continually focus on my husband's good traits, my thinking began to change. (Psychologists now realize that when a person's thinking changes, his or her feelings also change).

"Fresh love and appreciation for Bob began to spring up. Within three weeks we went away for a weekend trip and determined to take the necessary steps to make our relationship work. That was the beginning of the turnaround in our marriage.

"It has been over twenty-five years since that fateful day. Bob and I have a vibrant, happy, fun-filled, and fulfilling marriage and are more in love than ever before. We have five wonderful children and a van full of grandkids.

"Several things contributed to the turnaround in my marriage. The first was my decision to turn to God for help. Second was my desire to save — not escape from — my marriage. Third was my decision to counterbalance the negatives I was seeing in my husband with a focus on his good points. I realized that I was married to a good man. However, most of all was my decision to focus on the good.

"Bob and I would never have had a second chance at love except for my tearful decision to resurrect dead love by choosing to become a person of good report."

Noted author and radio commentator Dr. James Dobson describes this problem occurring in many marriages when "the wife concentrates on the missing elements and permits it to dominate their relationship. She's married to a good man — but he's not good enough."[1]

MAKE YOUR OWN HEADLINE

How many things can you itemize on a good report list of your spouse, parents, or key business associates? Do people feel good about themselves in your presence?

...whatsoever things are of good report...think on these things.
Philippians 4:8

R eal success must be viewed as a continuing sequence of events, not a one-time event.

In order to ensure continued success, planning and preparing for the future must be made even while maximizing the present.

This fact is manifested on a personal level when an individual makes delayed gratification a part of his living thought pattern.

This is not easy to do, especially in the midst of society's current dominant thought pattern expressed in the phrase "I want mine now."

Those who fail to adopt delayed gratification thinking normally find themselves fighting reoccurring battles with debt, marital problems, health difficulties, and relationship breakups.

Instead of spending all of their income, wise personal planners choose to set aside a certain amount for investment, future purchases, or savings.

This long-term thought process must also be a vital part of corporate strategy, as evidenced by a situation in the life of...

LEE IACOCCA

Soon after Lee Iacocca engineered one of the greatest turnarounds in industrial history at the Chrysler Corporation, a reporter asked him why, in the midst of astronomical cash shortages, asset liquidation, massive layoffs, and possible bankruptcy, he set aside $750 million to launch a new product —the Caravan.

He replied, "I had to. If you eat the seed corn, you have no future."[1]

Microsoft founder and president Bill Gates believes that this philosophy is one of his "power points" of success. He states: "The key trade-off is how much money to put into future improvement versus how much to put into present consumption. Keeping my money in productive investments suits me."[2]

In the Bible, throughout the four gospels, Jesus taught on the importance of this long-term thinking strategy. He knew that most people are short-sighted and focus on the present fruit rather than on future harvests. By teaching on the importance of planting and nourishing seed, Jesus endeavored to put people's mindset on a continuum of harvests rather than on one-time events.

If you desire to live a lifestyle of increase, you must determine to set aside — on a regular basis, regardless of circumstances — a certain amount of your present time, money, and energy as seed for future harvests and benefits.

MAKE YOUR OWN HEADLINE

Which of your activities would change if you truly focused on the seeds you are planting for the future, rather than on the harvests of today? How would this change affect your spending habits?

Except a seed fall into the ground...it cannot bring forth fruit.
John 12:24 (author's paraphrase)

LES BROWN

"When you want something so badly that you refuse to let go, you will probably get it," says Les Brown.

Of all the speakers with whom I share the stage, probably none is more alive and energetic than my friend Les Brown. More than that, he has the incredible ability to transfer his enthusiasm and energy to his audience.

He believes success-oriented people develop a powerful force that enables them to overcome obstacles and live out their dreams. He calls this force "hunger"!

Les believes that "when a person gets discouraged, and they will, it takes hunger to develop the courage to try again and again and never quit. Some people are naturally hungry. Others are not hungry enough."

I define hunger as a powerful determination — a consuming desire. It is not dependent upon your being in a situation of lack. It is a mindset that can be created, fed, and increased in intensity from whatever state or condition you may be in.

Les says, "If you want to increase this force, I can help. I'm a good cook."

LES BROWN'S HUNGER RECIPE

powerful reason to get up and fight back in life."
— Les Brown

1. TAKE RESPONSIBILITY FOR YOUR LIFE: Stop blaming other people and past negative circumstances for where you are. It is up to you to accomplish your dreams.

2. READ AND LISTEN: Consume tapes and inspirational material, such as the biographies of great people. Learn how they overcame great odds to succeed and how they achieved their goals.

3. DEVELOP A SENSE OF URGENCY: Take actions now that will move you toward your goals.

4. GET AROUND SUCCESSFUL PEOPLE: Find out what motivates them. Pick up their attitudes.

5. REVIEW YOUR GOALS: Twice every day read them and stay focused on achieving them.

6. DEVELOP COURAGE: Overcome your fears. Push them aside. Unmask them and then master them.

7. CONTEMPLATE YOUR MORTALITY: Predict the accomplishments you desire to achieve by the end of life. Write your obituary. Are you satisfied with what you put down?

8. PUSH YOURSELF: Operate on a massive, relentless scale in order to accomplish your goals.[1]

Les believes, "With a powerful hunger for your dreams driving you, you will be surprised at the ideas that will come, at the people you will be able to attract, and at the opportunities that will unfold."

Could you be doing more to increase your hunger for success? What is keeping you from pursuing your dreams? Are you talking enthusiastically about what you want to do with your life?

Blessed are they that hunger for they shall be fed.
Matthew 5:6 (author's paraphrase)

Freezing Gophers Shake Up School

Custodians at a California elementary school have learned how not to solve a gopher problem.

The custodians trapped some gophers that had been burrowing around the schoolyard. At first they were going to kill them by whacking them on the head with a hammer. Wanting to use a more humane method they decided to freeze the gophers to death by spraying them with gum remover, a product designed to be sprayed on the wads of gum found on the underside of school desks. The product freezes the gum, making it easier to chip off.

School officials state that, apparently, as the janitors were spraying the gophers one of the workers decided to light a cigarette. The fumes from the gum remover exploded, blowing the three custodians out of the utility room, and injuring a total of 19 people.

According to the police department, the gophers lived, and were taken into custody.

GETTING RID OF "GOPHERS"

As an achiever, one of the most difficult situations you will have to deal with is how to properly terminate a relationship with someone who has "burrowed into" your personal life and/or business.

In the handling of personal relationships it is normally desirable to maintain future friendship and good will.

In the case of an employee, it is not enough that you must deal with federal and state regulations. You must also be concerned with the possibility of a lawsuit and physical or verbal assault on you or your business. Therefore, proper handling in these termination situations is a must.

Five basic principles should be your guiding beacons:

"One of the most difficult situations you will have to deal with is how to properly terminate a relationship."
— Bob Harrison

TERMINATION PRINCIPLES

1. PRESERVE THE PERSON'S SELF-IMAGE: Separate rejection of job performance from rejection of the person.

2. DEMONSTRATE A CARING ATTITUDE: Be concerned about the person's feelings, well being, and future.

3. BE DISCREET: Be careful not to say things that will hurt the person or open you to future legal problems.

4. KEEP RECORDS: Keep records of any unsatisfactory work, criticisms, warnings, or important job performance reviews in case of possible future legal action.

4. BE CHRISTLIKE: As in everything you do, demonstrate the love of Jesus toward the person by treating him or her the way you would want to be treated if your roles were reversed.

Learn a lesson from the janitors with the gophers: An improperly handled termination can turn into an explosive situation!

MAKE YOUR OWN HEADLINE

How can you better terminate relationships? How can you better merge these four principles into your termination policy?

"...do to others what you would have them do to you...."
Matthew 7:12 NIV

Lightning Strikes Man On Golf Course

Knocked off his feet and stunned, the golfer quickly jumped up and noticed his friend wasn't breathing. He began performing CPR until paramedics arrived. Afterwards the victim said, "He gave me the gift of life."

You can give "the gift of life" to other people. It may not be by physically giving them air, but by speaking life into their dreams and self-images. It may be only a word or a note of encouragement.

A school teacher released this force into the life of...

RICH DEVOS

Rich DeVos is a champion in the "arena of Christian leaders." Not only is he the chairman and co-founder of Amway Corporation, but he is also president of a successful, professional basketball team, the Orlando Magic.

DeVos says, "One of the greatest things you can give to another person is the Gift of Encouragement. It is a gift with starting power, and staying power."

A school teacher released this gift into his life.

"One of the greatest gifts you can give to another person is the Gift of Encouragement."
— Rich DeVos

"When I was struggling to find my way as a high school senior, my Bible teacher sent me to a life of significance just by writing a few words in my yearbook, 'With talents for leadership in God's Kingdom.'

"The power of those seven words shook me. They jumped off the page and into my soul. They encouraged me to believe that God had a plan for me and my gifts.

"That note was written to me more than a half-century ago, but it remains fresh even today. With those words echoing in my ears I became determined to make a difference in life."

Zig Ziglar believes that the ability to encourage is a key ingredient in effective management. He says, "If you can catch people doing something well, no matter how small it may seem, and positively reinforce them for doing it, they will continue to grow in a positive direction."[1]

Jesus was an encourager. He would constantly praise His staff members and tell them, "Well done." He would praise others as well, such as the centurion who asked Jesus to heal his servant just by speaking the word. In front of everyone, Jesus boldly stated, "...I have not found so great faith, no, not in Israel" (Matthew 8:10).

Tom Peters says, "We wildly underestimate the power of the tiniest personal touch."[2]

The late Norman Vincent Peale stated, "When you encourage others, you fill your own heart with courage."[3]

You can also help others and be a blessing. Release the gift of encouragement into their lives.

How many different ways can you release encouragement into the life of others? Who could you write to or phone this week and give a "boost of encouragement" to their life? When was the last time you publicly encouraged someone?

"...Be of good courage."
Isaiah 41:6

When asked by reporters if he was trying to buy the election, Ross Perot exclaimed, "I'm buying it for people because they can't afford it. The politicians have made it too expensive."

In that statement, Perot showed his mastery of a debate and sales technique referred to as "reframing." I define it as changing a negative statement into a positive one, or vice versa, by changing the frame of reference used to perceive or interpret the experience.

The technique of reframing is based upon the fact that people do not necessarily see things the way they really are, but rather as they interpret or perceive them to be. Change that interpretation or perception, and you change people's reponse.

Here are some examples of reframing:

"My doctor is very considerate," a patient explained. "He tells me he is raising his fees so I can reach my deductible faster."

A man who forgot his wife's birthday got himself out of the jam by exclaiming: "How do you expect me to remember your birthday when you never look any older?"

Overcoming resistance or gaining favor by the use of reframing is a technique that can produce increased sales. It may even provide a way out of a delicate situation.

Note the following true story...

"DON'T YOU TRUST ME, DAD?"

My wife Cindy and I highly value our children. For that reason, we have never allowed any of them to go out on blind dates or to date strangers. This is particularly true with our daughters, who might be more vulnerable. We want to know they are with men of character, men who value their own reputations as well as those of our girls.

One Saturday several years ago, my oldest daughter Sandra was working in the front yard with us. Two young men, strangers to me, drove up and talked to her from their car at the foot of the driveway. After several minutes she came over to me and asked if she could go out with them that night.

I told her that I had never met the boys and knew nothing about them. (Besides not knowing them, I was also unimpressed that they did not get out of the car and introduce themselves to me). I suggested that she invite them to our family dinner outing the next week, so we could get to know them.

Her face turned red, and her eyes popped wide as she exclaimed, "What's wrong, don't you trust me, Dad?"

Knowing that I had to change her negative viewpoint, my reframing mindset immediately went to work.

I said, "Honey, if I had a million dollars in a briefcase, would I let some stranger borrow it for the evening?"

"Of course not," she replied.

"It's not that I don't trust you," I explained. "It's just that I'm trying to protect you. To Mom and me, you — and your future — are more valuable than a million dollars in a briefcase."

Her eyes became teary. She reached out her arms, hugged me, and said, "Thank you, Dad, for loving and caring for me so much."

By effectively using the technique of reframing, I quickly changed a negative situation into a positive one.

As an achiever, the ability to reframe is a talent that you should have in your verbal arsenal. The secret is to train your mind not just to think in terms of countering a disagreement, argument, or misunderstanding, but instead to change the context or frame of reference in which the situation is viewed by the other party.

As evidenced by the situation with my daughter, if you change the way a person thinks about something, you can automatically change how he or she feels about it.

MAKE YOUR OWN HEADLINE

What negative situations-perceptions are you encountering that could be turned around by the use of reframing? How can reframing improve your life?

...[Jesus said], "He that is without sin among you, let him first
cast a stone at her."
John 8:7

Kids Sue Father

Eleven-year-old twins have slapped their father with a lawsuit, because he doesn't spend any time with them.

This incident really happened. As part of a divorce settlement, the father was to see the boys every other weekend. However, he hadn't shown up in a year and a half. He had even had his phone programmed to block their calls, so the boys sued.

ABSENTEE FATHERS

This is a crisis in America. Kids raised in single-parent homes often struggle for identity, attention, and stability. They also lack the companionship and mentorship that can be gained from being around a caring dad.

T. D. Jakes says, "Many youth are living in anger and in pain, wondering what they did to drive away their daddy. A father's absence leaves kids desperately looking for someone else to 'fill in the blank.' Like a puzzle whose pieces can never create a full picture of their identity, there always seems to be a part missing."[1]

"I made a big mistake. I left my family too much. If I could do it again I would spend more time with them."

— Billy Graham

However, a different kind of "absentee father problem" is sweeping our land and affecting the families of many achievers.

Noted author and radio commentator James Dobson illustrates this crisis with a story about a little four-year-old who asks his playmate, "Where is your daddy? I never see him at your house."

The other boy replies, "Oh, he doesn't live here, he just sleeps here."[2]

A key advisor to President Bill Clinton walked away from his White House job after his ten-year-old son wrote him the following note:

"Baseball's not any fun when there is no one to applaud."

Success-oriented people don't need to become careerless to be good parents, but they must make family a priority.

Lee Iacocca, former chairman of the Chrysler Corporation, spent his evenings and Sundays at home with the family when he was in town. He felt that his job took up enough time without his having to shortchange his children.[3]

Iacocca stated, "Of all the jobs I've had in my life, none has been more important to me than my job as a dad. I've always felt that when I die, if I can say I've done well by my family, then I've lived a full and good life."[4]

In contrast, the son of a prominent national minister had a tearful reunion with his father in jail. The son repented of a rebellious lifestyle and drugs, saying, "I've spent my whole life trying to get your attention."

One secret to avoiding this priority pitfall is to schedule family time the same as business appointments are scheduled. In addition, when you are with your family members, don't just place your physical body in their presence. Let them also have your mind.

Must your children, grandchildren, and/or spouse fight to get your time and attention? What priority do you place on family?

...a child left to himself bringeth his mother [or father] to shame.
Proverbs 29:15

Beware Of Exploding Patients

A medical warning has been issued to doctors about patients who might explode during surgery. This rare occurrence can take place if nitrous oxide, which is sometimes used as an anesthetic in stomach surgery, mixes with the patient's intestinal gases and is accidentally ignited by a spark from electrical surgical instruments.

I have had some experience with "exploding patients," but they weren't in surgery. They had an anger problem.

Anger in itself is neither good nor bad. It is just an emotion. Whether it is a problem or not depends upon how and where the emotion is released.

Television football analyst John Madden teaches, "Never let your anger take hold of you. Turn it into aggressive action."

There are socially acceptable ways of displaying anger, such as throwing darts, hitting a punching bag, or cleaning house. Playing competitive sports is another acceptable form of release.

However, problems occur when anger is released in an unacceptable manner. Unbridled outbursts can create barriers of fear and intimidation in relationships, can result in the sowing of long-lasting hurts, and can negatively affect the health and image of the individual concerned.

An example of the wrong way to handle anger can be found with the former football coach of the University of Michigan. He had to resign from his job after an emotional outburst during which he allegedly punched a police officer.

There is another way, as described by...

TIM LAHAYE

He is a noted author and speaker who teaches on anger control. Here are some suggestions from his book titled *Anger Is a Choice*:

1. GET MORE INFORMATION: Information can change thoughts and feelings. Oftentimes what is perceived or assumed is not really happening at all.

2. OPEN YOUR MEMORY FILE: Hurt and anger from past experiences can continue to affect you now. Identify these. Don't let them trigger you.

3. EVALUATE: Are there common times, people, or associations that "trigger" your outbursts? If so, learn to avoid or be careful in these situations.

4. FACE YOUR ANGER: Trying to justify it, explain it, or blame someone else makes you incurable. You are responsible for your actions.

5. EXPRESS IT SOONER: Don't let negative feelings fester. Get over situations sooner. Express yourself before anger takes hold.

6. THINK POSITIVELY: The mind must dwell on something, so feed it positive emotional food.

7. RECOGNIZE DISPLACED ANGER: Most of the time people are angry about one thing but take our their anger on others who are not connected to it. Discover the real root cause of your anger.

8. CONFESS AND REPENT: When you do "lose it," ask forgiveness of the people involved and of God.

LaHaye concludes, "Anger is a habit...that can control a person as tenaciously as heroin or cocaine making them react inwardly and outwardly in a selfish manner."

He continues, "You need not remain a slave to this or any other habit. We have at our disposal the power of the Spirit of God to help us."[1]

Pat Riley, successful NBA coach, says, "Bad behavior patterns will always try to return and prevail. You simply have to know your style of backsliding and catch it as early as possible and turn it around."[2]

MAKE YOUR OWN HEADLINE

In what constructive ways can you better express your anger? Are there common times, people, or associations that "trigger" your outbursts?

...he that ruleth his spirit [is better] than he that taketh a city.
Proverbs 16:32

Cadillac Crashes Into Home

A local woman was suddenly awakened when a car crashed into her bedroom after knocking over a stop sign, jumping the curb, and skidding across her lawn.

The desire for a Cadillac in her driveway — not in her bedroom — changed a housewife's life. It caused her to begin a frantic search for uniqueness and knowledge in order to gain wealth and fame.

DR. JOYCE BROTHERS

In 1955, "The $64,000 Dollar Question," a popular quiz show, was the hottest program on television. On Tuesday nights, everyone watched the efforts of contestants to win the top prize, which was a fortune at that time. The more Joyce Brothers watched it, the more she thought, "I could do that."[1]

She did not even dream of winning the $64,000 prize. Her goal was to win the smaller prize — a Cadillac.

She analyzed the show. All the contestants were similar only in one respect — a built-in congruity in their life. For instance, there was a shoemaker who knew all about opera and a burly Marine who was a gourmet cook.

Then she analyzed her own situation. She was short, blonde, and pretty — a psychologist — and the mother of an almost-three-year-old. There was nothing paradoxical about her, nothing that would catch the attention of the powers-that-be who chose the show's contestants.

After some thought, she decided to become an expert on boxing. That would be sufficiently incongruous with her image to attract attention.

She states, "I went to work to turn myself into a boxing expert. I ate, drank, and slept boxing, its history, its statistics, its personalities.

"When I felt I was ready, I applied to be on the show and was accepted. I went on and won. I came back and won again. I kept on winning until...I won the Cadillac. That wasn't all...I continued winning until I also won...$64,000.

"That event changed my life. Soon I was on television and radio programs. I was making personal appearances. I was in show business. My career took off!"[2]

Superior knowledge was one of the secrets in the success of the ministry of Jesus Christ. As a young lad at the age of twelve, He was found by His parents in the temple sharing with the religious leaders. The Bible says that "...all that heard him were astonished at his understanding and answers" (Luke 2:47).

Harvey Mackay says, "The most powerful weapon anyone can possess in any negotiations is superior information and knowledge."[3]

Ted Nichols, author of more than 53 books, exclaims, "Today personal power comes from the possession and control of knowledge."

Possessing knowledge might not win you a luxury car or launch you on a worldwide ministry, but it will release blessings and increase in your life.

How much time are you actively spending increasing your knowledge?
What are you currently learning that is new and refreshing?

[God says] "My people are destroyed for lack of knowledge...."
Hosea 4:6

Periodic "pressure checks" should not only be a regular part of a person's physical routine, but also a part of his marital routine, as discovered by...

BILL McCARTNEY

He accomplished the seemingly impossible — by turning around a fledgling football program at Colorado University. Before he arrived as head coach, the team had won only seven games in the previous three years. By the time he resigned to devote his life full-time to a men's service organization called Promise Keepers, the team had been to nine post-season games in ten years, had been nationally ranked six years in a row, and had won a national championship.

However, during these years his great career successes had been offset by problems that developed on the home front as evidenced by what his wife Lyndi revealed in Bill's book *From Ashes to Glory*....

I Was A Wounded Woman

"After thirty years of marriage, you collect a lot of memories...some good and some bad. We were going through some bad times, and I was only seeing the bad stuff.

"I was hopelessly caught, eyebrow deep, in pain and blind to all the good of our marriage...I was a wounded woman.

"I needed answers. I read more than a hundred books in one year...books on recovery, on healing and on restoration. More importantly I read the Bible constantly.

"We went to a counselor...and later we got into a Bible study group — and it proved to be a time of real ministering...."

"During this time of inner conflict I went on a recruiting trip with Bill. There I was very honest with him as all the words and negative emotions I'd been bottling up came gushing out. It was very painful for both of us...but it began to cause change."[1]

Bill heard his wife's words and felt her pain. When he realized his shortcomings and how distant he had become, he begged God for forgiveness. He also determined to be a more sensitive and caring husband and father, and a more fruitful witness for the Lord.

Soon their marriage began to experience fresh love, joy, and excitement. Now, through the Promise Keeper publications and rallies and his personal life, Bill is committed to encouraging other men to do as he did — see their shortcomings, confess and repent of them, and turn their lives and marriages around.

If your mate and family members were asked to describe their feelings for you, what would they say? What are three ways that you can show love to your mate?

_____

Confess your faults one to another, and pray for one another, that ye may be healed....
James 5:16

_____

Man Comes Out Of Coma
After Seven Years

A Tennessee policeman, who was shot in the head while responding to a trouble call, is talking again.

I can appreciate the above story because my son Rock was in a coma when he was a little boy. The only difference is that Rock was in a "learning coma." He just could not learn to read.

Even though he was bright and did well in most subjects, he had great difficulty with reading. Because of his deficiency, he was required to repeat the first grade.

His reading difficulties continued in second grade. In early spring of that year, school officials called and asked my wife to come in for a conference. They informed her that Rock's reading was still at pre-school level, and that as a result they planned to make him repeat second grade again.

That night Cindy and I discussed his plight. Rock was already the biggest and oldest boy in his class. We felt that holding him back another year could create a rejection, stigma, and image problem that would negatively affect his self-image the rest of his life. We were frustrated

"Once a person's self-image improves, you will see significant gains in achievement."
— Denis Waitley

and disappointed, but didn't know what to do. Rock had begun to see himself as a failure.

Dr. Maxwell Maltz, author of a bestselling book on psychocybernetics, says, "All of a person's actions...feelings...behavior...and even abilities... are always consistent with their self-image. They will 'act like' the person they conceive themselves to be."[1]

Denis Waitley says, "Once a person's self-image improves, you will see significant gains in achievement."

While in prayer together one night, we felt impressed by God to use these insights on self-image as the foundation for a change in our son.

We activated the following...

STRATEGY FOR SUCCESS

1. PRAISE: We began to praise Rock for all his past and current accomplishments and subjects in which he was doing well.

2. LOVE: We reaffirmed to him that our love and acceptance was not based upon his performance, but rather on his relationship to us.

3. TIME: We rearranged our schedules so we could give him extra time for play, personal attention, and reading assistance.

4. AFFIRMATION: Since belief can be established by repetition, we made him confess daily several times 1 John 4:4: "Greater is He that is in me, than he that is in the world." In addition, several times a day we would make him boldly proclaim, "I AM A WINNER!"

SHOCKING NEWS!

Almost immediately, we began to see improvement in his attitude and ability to read. However, none of us was ready for the shock that would soon come.

Several weeks later, school officials contacted us to say that they were absolutely astonished at Rock's improvement. He had "skyrocketed" from pre-school reading level to mid-year third grade level in less than 90 days.

Not only was Rock allowed to advance to the next grade, but on the last day of school, he won the award for being the number one reader in his class!

MAKE YOUR OWN HEADLINE

Who could use your praise, love, time, and admiration in order to develop a better self-image? What could you be doing to develop a winning attitude in that person's life? What steps can you take to improve your own self-image and corresponding achievement?

Therefore encourage one another and build each other up....
1 Thessalonians 5:11 NIV

Toilet Paper Puts Squeeze On Principal

Police used a marked roll of toilet paper to catch a principal who was stealing bathroom tissue from his school. The markings, which could only be seen under ultraviolet light, were put on the paper by the police after a school janitor reported that he noticed rolls were routinely missing from a supply room after the principal ate his lunches there.

Here is an example of a person who went through intensive training and preparation to obtain a position of leadership, only to see his career go "down the drain." As with many others, while succeeding in academic training, he apparently failed in character training.

The dictionary defines character as distinctive traits or behavior that is typical of a person.

Character is a learned behavior. It is best taught at a young age by precept and example at home, as illustrated by...

JESS GIBSON

He is an incredible motivational speaker, pastor, and friend from Springfield, Missouri. He shares about one of his tests of character as a young boy.

"At the age of 15, I had a before-school job at a pharmacy. One morning I was sweeping behind the counter where the cash register sat. All of a sudden I saw it.

"A beautiful crisp $10 bill was laying there, just waiting for me to pick it up. The boss was in the basement. No one else was in the store. Who would know? Should I or shouldn't I?

"Crisis does not develop character, but reveals it."
— Jess Gibson

"What could I do with $10? Visions of candy and sugar plums danced through my head! Then it dawned on me. My trustworthiness, my character, was being tested. My actions at that precise moment would shed light on who I really was and who I would become.

"I picked up the money, ran to the basement, and presented it proudly to the owner. He didn't even say thanks, but grumbled that someone had been clumsy handling money.

"However, I had my reward in that the experience revealed to me that I had developed the character traits that would help guide me throughout life, and enable me to overcome bigger challenges and temptations."[1]

Each action you take when faced with moral questions or temptations will help form your habits, which in turn will determine your character.

MAKE YOUR OWN HEADLINE

What character traits do you need to focus on in order to make your private life consistent with your public life? What are your deep-down-in-the-heart values?

But [we] have renounced the hidden things of dishonesty...
commending ourselves to every man's conscience in the sight of God.
2 Corinthians 4:2

Years ago I was introduced to a book which for me has become "The Real Thing." It is called the Bible.

I discovered that it contains secret ingredients which, when applied to one's life, can help eradicate doubt, unbelief, fear, and loneliness. These ingredients include faith, hope, love, wisdom, and supernatural endowments that empower people to reach the full potential God has planned for their lives.

The fake substitutes or counterfeits of the Bible that are currently being marketed are religious teachings and/or writings that ignore and/or contradict Biblical truths. In place of personal relationship with God and living according to Biblical principles, these teachings substitute programs that only offer self-mastery through inner meditation.

These "self-improvement" programs do contain some valid truths. However, when they are implemented to the exclusion of a Biblical foundation they will normally leave a person "feeling better" with transient excitement but still lacking in real power and guidance.

An individual can only achieve his or her greatest potential by possessing the "internal armor" and stability that come from a life committed to Biblical principles.

Following are some of my personal keys for using "The Real Thing":

HOW TO USE "THE REAL THING"

1. STAND ON TRUTH: Commit yourself, and all that you are, to the fact that the Bible is true.

2. SEPARATE: Set aside a quiet time and place for the purpose of praying, reading the Bible, and contemplating its truths.

3. MEDITATE: Don't fall into the trap of just "quick reading" a certain number of pages per day. If a particular verse or story has meaning to you, stop and meditate and maybe even memorize the key verses.

4. VERBALLY AFFIRM WHAT GOD IS DOING: The key to receiving from God is to make your mouth agree with what God says. Confess aloud what the Bible says you are and what God will do for and through you.

5. BE PATIENT: Patience is the quality that does not surrender to circumstances or succumb under trial. Possess the wisdom of a farmer who knows that it takes time for seed to become a harvest.

6. RESIST DOUBT: Refuse to be moved by what you see, hear, or feel, or by what others say if it contradicts what the Bible teaches.

7. FIGHT FEAR: Fear is the strongest enemy of faith, and faith is the environment for spiritual victories. Train yourself to answer empty threats of fear with quotes from God's Word.

Television pastor Charles Stanley also emphasizes the importance of a Bible-based life: "Nothing motivates me like seeing people integrate the principles of God's Word into their lives."[1]

I encourage you not to be satisfied with "religious counterfeits." In order to release God's power for victory in your life, you must know and use "The Real Thing." It is called the Bible.

MAKE YOUR OWN HEADLINE

What are you doing on a weekly basis to absorb Biblical principles into your mind? How are you applying and activating its hidden ingredients into your daily routine?

...be not conformed to this world [and its way of thinking]: but be ye
transformed by the renewing of your mind....
Romans 12:2

More Kids Minus Fathers

The number of children living without fathers has quadrupled from 6 percent to 24 percent since 1950.

GEORGE AND BARBARA BUSH

My wife and I were invited to a special luncheon in Tampa, Florida, with former President George Bush and his wife, Barbara. It was a memorable experience to sit and talk with two of the world's most respected leaders.

President Bush was raised in a Christian home where prayer and regular church attendance were the norm. He is a believer who refers to Rev. Jerry Falwell, Rev. Charles Stanley, and Rev. Billy Graham as his friends.

When asked what he perceived to be the most difficult problem facing America today, he replied...

"THE MOST SERIOUS PROBLEM FACING AMERICA IS THE DECLINE OF THE TRADITIONAL FAMILY."

There are things one can do to help reverse this destructive trend, such as giving financial assistance to family-oriented ministries and charities

"Family must come first."
— George Bush

and supporting political candidates who espouse traditional family values.

However, the most important thing anyone can do is keep his or her own marriage strong.

According to a recent Roper Organization Survey, the five qualities that women value most for a satisfying marriage are:

1. Mutual love

2. Respect

3. Friendship

4. Shared values

5. Sexual satisfaction

Keep these areas of your marriage strong and you will not be a part of the problem, but a part of the answer.

MAKE YOUR OWN HEADLINE

How can you improve your relationship with your spouse in each of the above areas? How can you better show your spouse that you love him/her?

Submitting yourselves one to another in the fear of God.
Ephesians 5:21

$60,000 In New Bills Missing

The Bureau of Engraving and Printing reported that someone figured out how to breach its security.

Over a period of thirty days $60,000 was stolen from under the noses of the people who print the nation's currency.

Is it possible that you have areas in your personal and/or business life in which you are vulnerable to breaches of security? If so, it could cost you money, as evidenced by a story out of the pages of *Automotive Age*.

A worried Toyota dealer placed an urgent call to Bill Ellis, president of a sales audit company. In panic, the harried dealer exclaimed: "WE ARE SHORT $90,000 DOLLARS IN INVENTORY."

Bill immediately scheduled an appointment at the dealership to review the records of its service department. He found that several sales tickets for automotive parts were missing. In fact, more than a thousand tickets were missing. He then discovered that an employee who sold parts was throwing away numerous cash sales tickets each week and pocketing the money.

The amazing thing was that the dealership had instituted a program to prevent this kind of theft. A dedicated and loyal employee had been assigned to keep a missing ticket log.

"People do
what is
inspected, not
what is
expected."
— Bob Harrison

Then how did this loss occur? Unbelievable as it may seem, the employee had never been instructed why the list was being kept, or what to do when tickets were missing. She just faithfully noted the missing ticket numbers without ever notifying anyone or doing anything about them.

Fresh with the memory of this embezzlement, over the next sixty days, Bill audited more than a hundred other dealerships, specifically checking for missing parts sales tickets. To his surprise he found the following:

ARE YOU INVITING THEFT?

- one-third of the dealerships had the same person who received cash from the customers keeping track of missing tickets.

- one-sixth of them kept no record of ticket numbers at all.

And most amazing, not one of the hundred dealerships audited had checked their missing ticket log in the previous three months.[1]

All of these businesses were inviting theft or embezzlement because they either did not have, or did not maintain, a proper inspection system.

You may think that you could never have this kind of problem, but even Jesus did.

John 12:6 states that Judas, who was the treasurer of the disciples, "...was a thief, and had the bag [money], and bare [stole] what was put therein." If Jesus was susceptible to embezzlement, then so are you.

As any student of effective time management knows, it is impossible to grow to full potential without delegating certain functions to others. No one individual can do and watch everything.

However, if you expect to truly succeed in any enterprise, you had better be diligently and regularly inspecting your key areas of income, expenses, and cash flow.

What systems do you have in place to protect the key areas of income, expenses, cash flow, customer data, and inventory? How often are you inspecting those systems?

Riches can disappear fast...so watch your business interests closely.
Proverbs 27:23,24 TLB

Achievers Told To Make A Difference

God, business, country, and family blended together at the Free Enterprise Convention that attracted 26,000 distributors to Knoxville this weekend.

I will never forget walking on stage to the clapping, yelling, and whistling of the enthusiastic throng that had filled the University of Tennessee basketball arena that August day in 1990. It was a "highlight time" for me in my career as a motivational speaker.

Another high point was the opportunity to listen to and get acquainted with one of the world's top marketing geniuses who was also on the speaking program.

DEXTER YAGER

Although his multi-million-dollar worldwide networking business is still the hub of his income-making activities, Dexter Yeager also owns and operates a long list of businesses and real estate developments.

He and his charming wife Birdie note that their lives changed when they read a positive-thinking book and saw the need to develop fresh goals and new dreams.

Dexter says that "to succeed you must set goals and then claim them as if they are already yours. When you work towards those goals and dreams as if there is no way you could not get them, you will succeed."

Here are some of...

DEXTER YAGER'S SUCCESS SECRETS

1. LEARN WHAT TO DO FROM THE BEST: Seek out those people who know what they're doing and who have performed consistently over time.

2. PRACTICE: In front of anyone at anytime, practice as if your life depended on winning them over.

3. KEEP GETTING BETTER: Move to higher levels by constantly improving yourself.

4. MOTIVATE YOURSELF: Find five to ten things you can't live without. This will give you the energy and the drive to succeed.

5. WRITE DOWN YOUR DREAMS: Writing them makes them seem more practical, more immediate and less abstract. This is a vital element for success.

6. TOUCH YOUR DREAMS: At least once per week touch one of your dreams, whatever it is. If you have several, then pick one major one. Just seeing and touching your dreams helps you focus on your goals and stay motivated.

7. DIVIDE YOUR DREAMS INTO SMALLER ACHIEVABLE GOALS: Write down what you can do now to begin the process of achievement.

8. VISUALIZE YOURSELF HAVING REACHED YOUR GOAL: This is an incredibly powerful motivational force. It will activate you to overcome resistance.

9. Do More: Go the extra mile. Out-dream, out-work, and out-love everybody.

10. Pray: Work as though everything depends on you, and pray as though everything depends on God. It does.[1]

Dexter believes that if you will follow through on these points, you will have created a plan to fulfill your dreams.

MAKE YOUR OWN HEADLINE

Do you have a written success plan? In which items on Dexter's list of success secrets do you need improvement? Have you divided your dream into smaller achievable goals?

"For I know the plans I have for you," declares the Lord, "plans to prosper you and not to harm you, plans to give you hope and a future."
Jeremiah 29:11 NIV

Parents Made Kids Eat Rats And Roaches

Chicago police arrested the parents of four children who had been abused and fed boiled rats and deep-fried roaches.

The average person is appalled to read about such abuse by parents. Yet, I wonder how many parents feed their children verbal rats and roaches.

Many psychologists believe that if children (or spouses or employees) are continuously yelled at and told that they are dumb, clumsy, or unattractive, a negative self-image can be formed in their minds.

Probably more than anything else, the words of others form and shape an individual's self-image.

Just as the wrong diet of food can make one physically sick, the wrong diet of words can make one mentally and emotionally sick. It can also lead to sub-par performance.

Robert Schuller says, "A person's self-image will always reproduce itself in action."[1]

Zig Ziglar teaches, "If a person doesn't see himself as a winner, he cannot perform as a winner."[2]

One example of the relationship of self-image to performance can be found in the story of...

PETER DANIELS

He is an Australian real estate multi-millionaire, corporate advisor, and sought-after speaker. An event from his childhood provides a good illustration of the above truth. He shares it in his book, *Miss Phillips, You Were Wrong*.

"My teacher, Miss Phillips, thought that I WAS INATTENTIVE, DUMB, AND NAUGHTY.

"The real truth was I did not understand.

"One unforgettable day, I did try extremely hard and passed my work up to Miss Phillips with a certain amount of pride and satisfaction, expecting at the very least a comment of acceptance or maybe even an acknowledgment of good work before the whole class. But Miss Phillips thundered down between the desks toward me,... stood me up, shook me and punched my back and then...shook with all her strength, yelling, 'Peter Daniels, you are a bad, bad, boy and you are never going to amount to anything!'

"That event both crushed and angered me and was to dog me for the rest of my school years. It affected my attitude and ability to the point where it became, in a sense, a self-fulfilling prophecy."[3]

During his mid-twenties, a defeated and almost illiterate Peter Daniels attended a Billy Graham crusade and became a born-again Christian.

The realization that the Holy Spirit then resided in him changed his self-image and opened him up to a whole new life. It broke the power of fear off of him. He began to read and gain knowledge and confidence. Soon he went into business for himself and became very successful. Today he lives a lifestyle of wealth, privilege, and prestige. He lectures at great universities, is a consultant to industrial tycoons, and flies around the globe as a highly paid seminar and convention speaker.

Emergency crews in many cities possess a mechanical device called "the jaws of life." This tool can cut through doors, twisted wreckage, or just about anything in order to free trapped victims.

Your mouth is like that tool. It can be a powerful force of hope and encouragement, freeing victims trapped by poor self-images and negative circumstances.

Peter Daniels' life changed when an event changed his self-image. Your words can build up or tear down the images and dreams that others have of themselves. Determine that you are going to possess the "jaws of life."

MAKE YOUR OWN HEADLINE

What kind of "word food" are you giving to your children, spouse, or employees? How would a positive change of their "verbal diet" affect their self-image and future?

A word fitly spoken is like apples of gold in pictures of silver.
Proverbs 25:11

Governor To Say "Thanks" To Firms

The governor left on a two-day economic development trip to the Northeastern United States.

The purpose of the trip is to give him an opportunity to personally thank the executives of four major companies for their economic investments in the state.

Because of demanding schedules and the hustle of daily routines, it is easy to overlook the thoughtful, caring acts of others. Achievers, in particular, must be very careful not to fall into the "pit of thanklessness," because people respond to praise.

Effective achievers make gratitude a part of their motivational arsenal.

Here are...

THREE WAYS TO HELP SHOW APPRECIATION

1. SAY THANKS NOW: Form the habit of verbalizing appreciation the moment it is appropriate.

2. ACKNOWLEDGE THE CONTRIBUTIONS OF OTHERS: Give unexpected encouragement — gifts, flowers, or notes of appreciation — even when there is no special occasion.

3. CELEBRATE THE SUCCESS OF OTHERS: On special occasions do something a little extra for people.

Last Mother's Day, our youngest daughter Crystol wrote a special poem to show appreciation to her mom. Part of it went as follows:

THANK YOU, MOM

Mother, since your love is so special and so real,
I want to take a moment to tell you how I feel.

Your love brings the blue skies and wipes away my tears,
It gives me shelter and rids me of my fears.

The beauty of a flower is like your loving care,
Full of life and happiness your love is always there.

Your love is a comfort to me and your life is a guide,
Even when you are far away you are here by my side.

There is not another mom that could give a love so true,
And there is not a daughter who could love you like I do.

Bill Marriott, president of Marriott Hotels, says, "The two most important words in human relations are thank you."[1]

Zig Ziglar says, "If you will give everyone the recognition and rewards they deserve, both of you will have taken a giant step toward becoming top performers!"[2]

Power Point
"What you do not maintain and appreciate you will eventually lose." — Bob Harrison

MAKE YOUR OWN HEADLINE

How can you better show appreciation to those who have invested in your life or are helping you experience increase? When was the last time you complimented your family or staff members?

...be ye thankful.
Colossians 3:15

Swamp Survivor

A veteran outdoorsman was rescued after being lost in a Georgia swamp for forty-one days. He survived by eating bugs, leaves, and berries.

In order to enjoy continuing success, you must not only master conquering skills but also be able to survive through unexpected seasons of difficulty. This is true because life consists not only of seasons of increase, but also times of just surviving, as evidenced in the life of...

EDNA HARRISON-HARLIN

My mom had to survive in a season of despair after the sudden death of my father. She and my dad had been so close that when he died, it seemed to her that her joy and purpose for living was gone. She says, "In losing my husband, I felt like Job of old: I had lost everything."[1]

Mom not only personally worked her way out of her despair, but began to help others who were suffering from a loss. In the process she began an organization called New Lease On Life, which now has chapters around the world.

The purpose of New Lease is to help people who have lost a loved one through death, separation, or divorce. They are encouraged to grow by moving from aloneness to the security of individuality, based upon a relationship with Jesus Christ.

In her book, *A Second Chance at Love*, Mom shares her journey out of the swamp of despair.

MY MOM'S SWAMP-SURVIVAL COURSE

"God meets us at our point of weakness. In contrast to the philosophy of God helping those who help themselves, I found that oftentimes He helps those who can't help themselves.

"Trying to recover in our own strength leads to weariness and failure. As long as I focused on the 'I' rather than 'I AM,' I was disillusioned. The 'I' orientation eventually makes a person bitter instead of better. It takes a complete surrender to God in order to find peace with self.

"That is the turning point. Once I allowed Him to begin the resurrection in my life, God began to work in ways that were beyond my wildest dreams.

"The Lord was teaching me something important: Helping others would help me. It is a strange but proven Biblical principle, 'give and you shall receive.'"[2]

Today Mom is in her eighties, regularly swims forty laps in the pool, and is happily bringing hope and joy into the lives of others.

Mark Twain stated, "The best way to cheer yourself up is to cheer everybody else up."[3]

If you examine closely the heros and heroines of the Bible, you will observe that the common thread among them is simply that they troubled themselves to help others on God's behalf.

When my mother did that, her life changed for the better. So will yours.

How can you focus more on helping others and less on helping yourself? List three things that you can do this month to help those who are hurting.

...if you...satisfy the need of the afflicted, then shall your light rise in darkness, and your obscurity and gloom become like the noonday.
Isaiah 58:10 AMP

Surgery Removes Staph Infection

Quarterback Vinny Testaverde will remain hospitalized for three more days after having surgery to remove a staph infection in his leg. After cutting his shin during practice two weeks ago he developed the infection. Fortunately, the infection did not reach Testaverde's bloodstream. If it had it could have been fatal.

There is a different kind of "infection" that affects many churches, clubs, businesses, and families and may also be fatal.

This kind of infection normally begins when someone within the organization, group, or relationship becomes upset by some other member, situation, or perceived injustice. Instead of giving the situation time to change or correct itself, the disgruntled individual begins to manifest his or her negative feelings through criticism, disrespect, pouting, temper tantrums, or hostility.

If not handled quickly and properly by those in authority, this person's negative attitude can spread to others in the family, group, or business. When this occurs it is no longer a personal problem, but rather it becomes a "staff infection."

I refer to this "disease" by this title because it soon spreads beyond one person and begins to affect others. As with physical infection, if left

"If someone or something is negative, deal with the situation as quickly as possible."
— Bob Harrison

untreated it can be harmful to the harmony and unity of the business or family unit, and may prove fatal.

To prevent this from happening to you, in dealing with negative people and/or situations consider the following:

"STAFF INFECTION" TREATMENT KEYS

1. BE PROACTIVE: If you discover that someone or something is negative, deal with the situation as quickly as possible.

2. FIND THE ROOT CAUSE: Discover the root cause of the "disease" and try to deal with it rather than just reacting to its symptoms.

3. CONTAIN THE OUTBREAK: Recognize individual negativism as a contagious infection that needs to be treated while it is still localized and has not spread to others. Consider discussing with the person involved your concern about the dangers of his or her negative responses.

4. QUARANTINE THE INFECTED: Whenever possible, during the treatment process reduce or eliminate the exposure of others in the group to the person or persons spreading the "disease."

5. CHANGE THE ENVIRONMENT: In an effort to preserve the relationship, if possible change the responsibilities, location, or assignments of those involved.

6. COUNTERACT: Find any positive aspects of the person or situation being negatively affected. Publicize these positive points to the main group as part of an overall "cure."

6. PERFORM SURGERY: If all other treatment fails, make the changes needed to cut out the cause or — if necessary, the source and/or carrier of the negativism.

Throughout the Bible, prophets, and even Jesus Himself, had to remove negative people or remove themselves from negative situations before increase or miracles could be manifested.

Determine that you are not going to ignore personal negativism, but rather will deal with it in a firm but compassionate way before it infects others.

MAKE YOUR OWN HEADLINE

What negative attitudes or situations are you facing that are working against the achievement of your dreams? Have you allowed yourself to become personally negative about a situation or another person? What do you need to do to change or correct this situation or individual?

Now I beseech you, brethren, mark them which cause divisions
and offences contrary to the doctrine which ye have learned;
and avoid them.
Romans 16:17

After a 35-day book tour, 53,000 autographs, and three weeks of counsel and meditation, Colin Powell announced that he would not run for President.

GENERAL COLIN POWELL

When he was chairman of the Joint Chiefs of Staff, Gen. Colin Powell was known for how carefully he prepared for battle. He would order satellite photos, send out scouting patrols, and collect all the intelligence information available before deciding where, or whether, to attack.

He used this same strategy in making the decision whether or not to run for the office of president of the United States.

According to General Powell, the strategy is this: "Collect all the data you can, and if uncertain don't make the decision until you must."

This strategy is also found throughout the Bible. Before committing to war or major decisions, kings would often call in their advisors or seek counsel from the prophets of God.

INDECISION IS THE KEY TO FLEXIBILITY

I understand that one of the most important characteristics of all achievers is decisiveness: the ability to make tough decisions quickly. I also recognize that the delaying of decisions can create uncertainty and result in missed opportunities.

In every situation, there comes a crucial point when a decision must be made and then acted upon immediately.

On the other hand, sometimes deciding too quickly can lead to disastrous consequences.

In my own life experience I have learned that if I don't have all the facts, or do not feel at peace, unless a decision is required immediately, it is best to wait.

Until I commit to a decision, I retain the ability to change, adjust, modify, or explore further options. In many cases this flexibility has enabled me to discover better solutions, receive more favorable terms, avoid costly mistakes, and/or tremendously increase the impact of the right decision because of better timing.

In particular I have discovered that the timing of a decision is critical! The more opposition expected from a decision, the more important it is to carefully choose the right moment to make it — or reveal it.

The prime minister of Israel discovered this fact recently when he announced at the wrong time the decision to begin new excavations at Temple Mount. Riots and loss of life resulted.

Real estate tycoon Donald Trump uses the same mindset in decision making: "I am a firm believer in asking everyone for an opinion before I make a decision. I ask and ask and ask until I begin to get a gut feeling about it. That's when I make a decision."[1]

World War II general George Patton amplified this same decision-making strategy when he said, "If uncertain, delay the decision as long as possible so that more information can be collected. But when a decision must be made, don't hesitate."[2]

A great leader is not always the one who makes quick decisions, but the one who makes right decisions.

Are you losing flexibility, exercising poor timing, or making costly mistakes by forcing yourself to reach decisions too soon? What pending decisions should be delayed for better terms and/or timing?

Suppose one of you wants to build a tower. Will he not first sit down and estimate the cost to see if he has enough money to complete it?
Luke 14:28 NIV

GAVIN AND PATTI MACLEOD

They act like he is really the captain of "The Love Boat" and she is "The Princess." Every time Cindy and I are with them, socially or at a television studio, they radiate joy, happiness, love, and energy.

However, things have not always been that way for this charming couple. Several years ago, their own "love boat" ran aground on the rocks of divorce.

Patti says that it was worse than anything she had ever been through — worse than her father leaving the family when she was a little girl, worse than her mother's death.

There was no relief. For months on end, she felt pain twenty-four hours a day. She couldn't figure out why her husband had left. "What was wrong with her?" she wondered.

> "If we don't take time for each other, we will wind up in the same alienated predicament as before."
> — Gavin MacLeod

She found herself in confusion as to what to do. Her secular therapists all told her to forget him and get on with her life, while her Christian friends kept telling her that God is a "God of restoration."

Patti chose to believe that God would heal the broken relationship and began to earnestly pray for herself, her marriage, and her husband.

Silently, God began to move behind the scenes.

Not long after Patti began praying and believing, Gavin unexpectedly called to ask her to a social get-together. She suggested dinner at home. When Gavin arrived and stood in the doorway, she spoke her classic line, "Your dinner is a little cold. It's been waiting three years."

Soon thereafter, the "estranged couple" were remarried.

From their book, *Back on Course*, here are some of their suggestions for maintaining a great marriage:

GAVIN AND PATTI'S MARRIAGE SECRETS

1. CELEBRATE TOGETHERNESS: Go places together, meet friends together, make decisions together.

2. BE SENSITIVE: God sees you as partners. Promise each other that "your wants and needs are important to me."

3. GIVE EACH OTHER TIME: Set aside time for each other to do the things that each of you enjoy.

4. GIVE EACH OTHER SPACE: Don't try to possess or control all the other person's time or activities.

5. DISCUSS FEELINGS AND DESIRES: Don't clam up or stop talking. Communicate! Encourage each other to share.

6. PRAY TOGETHER: Take personal prayer time alone daily, but also have a devotional time together each day.[1]

By activating these keys as a foundation of their relationship, Gavin and Patti MacLeod are now enjoying smooth sailing on the sea of marriage. According to Patti, "We are more in love than ever before."

MAKE YOUR OWN HEADLINE

How many of the above secrets are you actively using in your marriage?

───────────────

...let every one of you...love his wife even as himself; and the wife see that she reverence her husband.
Ephesians 5:33

───────────────

The threat of death for mispronouncing someone's name is extreme. Even in America, remembering or correctly pronouncing a person's name can mean life or death — not in a physical sense but in regard to a relationship or a sale.

Therefore, it is important for success-oriented people to remember — and correctly pronounce — the names of people they meet and deal with.

Psychologists say that most memory problems are really due to what is termed "impression deficit." To guard against or overcome this deficiency and to increase your ability to remember names, try these...

THREE STEPS TO BETTER NAME RECALL

1. IMPRESSION: When meeting someone, concentrate your attention on the individual and his or her name.

2. REPETITION: Repeat the name by using it in the conversation as soon as practical. If possible, write it down.

3. ASSOCIATION: Attempt to visually associate the name to a place, event, or image.

For Christian achievers there is another helpful memory strategy. The Bible teaches that through prayer, the Holy Spirit will help bring things to remembrance.

If you experience a "memory blank," and the normal memory triggers aren't working, try this effective method: pray and ask God to help you.

Also, it is not enough just to remember names, but they must be pronounced correctly. Consider writing down difficult names phonetically to assist in later use.

DO THEY KNOW WHAT YOU MEAN?

In all communication it is critical that words be spoken clearly and that the receiving party comprehends the intended meaning. Imagine the problems of a medical doctor communicating with an ordinary lay person if the meaning of his terms was not understood:

Cesarean section: a neighborhood in Rome
Impotent: distinguished; well known
Labor pain: getting hurt at work
Nitrates: cheaper than day rates
Outpatient: a person who has fainted
Seizure: a famous Roman emperor
Terminal illness: airport sickness
Tumor: more than one
Ultrasound: a loud noise
Urine: opposite of "you're out"

In order to experience the upper levels of success, you must be an effective communicator. You must have a system to remember people's names and be certain your communications are clearly understood.

What systems can you develop to help you remember names better?

"But the Comforter, which is the Holy Ghost...he shall teach you all things, and bring all things to your remembrance...."
John 14:26

Economy Breaks Out Of Rut

The economy has broken out of its slow growth rut. Economists declare the recession finally over.

Your personal economic situation today is a reflection of the choices you have made to date. If you are dissatisfied with your current financial status and desire to change, the process begins with a decision to change your thinking, thereby changing your circumstances, and your level of living.

A perfect example is...

BILL SWAD

He is one of America's most successful automobile men. At one time, he simultaneously operated Ohio's largest Chevrolet, Chrysler, and Nissan dealerships, as well as a large automobile leasing company and finance company. But, he was not always that successful. His life changed when he made a decision.

He was a baggage handler at the local airport when he decided to get out of his economic rut. He determined to accomplish this goal by going into the used car business.

At a seminar in Tulsa he shared the story of his opening day experience:

"I borrowed $1000 from a loan company to purchase three used cars. I brought in a little gravel, hung a few light bulbs on a wire, and was ready for business. My sales 'shack' was like a little green house made out of orange crates and glass.

"I felt ten feet tall on the inside because I had made a total decision regarding my future and believed that I could do it.

"A postman stopped by with some junk mail that first morning. He told me about a flower business, a man who sold old 'memorabilia,' and others that had opened and closed at this same location. He said, 'Mister, you probably ought to know that several businesses have started on this corner and all of them failed.'

"I wasn't about to let his negative beliefs ruin my future. I looked at the mailman and boldly exclaimed, 'Well, mister, this business is going to succeed.'

"An hour later I had my first customer. I sold a Ford and took a Plymouth in on trade. I was off and running. The vehicles began selling faster than I ever imagined."

Within three years Bill was the biggest retail used car dealer in the state of Ohio. Next came his new car dealerships: AMC, Chrysler/Plymouth, Nissan, Lincoln/Mercury, Chevrolet, Cadillac, Buick, Pontiac, and GMC trucks. Then he added an insurance company, two mortgage companies, real estate developments, and more.

Bill succeeded because he was willing to take the risks, had a plan of action, was determined to overcome obstacles, and would not let the negative opinions of others deter him.

Fred Smith was a college student who also had a desire to succeed, and a plan. He even wrote out the details for a project at Yale University. His professor gave him a grade of "C," saying, "The concept is interesting and well-formed, but in order to earn better than a 'C' the idea must be feasible."[2]

Fred would not let this negative opinion deter him. He started his dream company anyway. It is named Federal Express.

Where did it all begin for these men? With a decision to succeed, to get out of the rut and move ahead with their dream.

MAKE YOUR OWN HEADLINE

Are you satisfied with your current lifestyle? What decisions can you make that will cause it to change for the better? Are you letting the negative opinions of others keep you from pursuing your dreams?

"...choose life, that both thou and thy seed may live."
Deuteronomy 30:19

Only four of America's ten major airlines are expected to make a profit in the fourth quarter this year, and two of them are discount carriers.

ROBERT CRANDALL

He is chairman of American Airlines. Under his leadership, American has broken out of the pack to become one of the world's two largest airlines.

He sat across the aisle from me on a recent flight to Tulsa. We had a wonderful talk about business in general and about the things I liked and didn't like about his company's AAdvantage Frequent Flyer Program and the carrier as a whole. I found it interesting that two of my suggestions were implemented by American within a few weeks of our flight together. One of the secrets of effective leaders is that they train themselves to listen.

I noticed another of Mr. Crandall's success secrets at work a few months ago when the news media reported that American was disposing of most of its fleet of jumbo jets and replacing them with smaller craft. When a reporter asked Mr. Crandall why he was doing this, he replied, "No airline has ever gone broke flying planes that are too small. Airlines go broke by flying planes that are too big."[1]

In this statement there is a powerful point to consider. Increase thinkers are always prepared to grow and expand as need demands, however...

THINKING INCREASE DOES NOT ALWAYS MEAN THINKING BIGGER

In the case of this airline, the term "increase thinking" means something quite different. AA's consumer surveys revealed that its flyers were more interested in the frequency of jet departures than in plane size. By flying smaller jets, the airline could increase flight frequency. Also, the company realized that it is a lot easier to fill smaller jets, resulting in higher load factors and correspondingly greater profits.

In my travels crisscrossing the nation, I have lost count of the number of times that I have consulted and prayed with some business leader or pastor who is in financial difficulty, solely because he built a facility that was too big and expensive or expanded overhead too quickly.

Jesus taught on this concept in John 15. He shared how a grapevine's long-term output was actually increased through pruning (cutting back) the branches. Because of this pruning, the branches that were left received more nourishment and strength from the roots, causing more and bigger fruit to be produced.

While increasing, you must be careful not to overextend yourself or your resources. Also, you must be ready to temporarily cut back in certain areas if it will result in greater future growth.

The age of the dinosaurs is over. This is as true in business and ministry as it is in history and science. Increase — and oftentimes survival — goes to the sleek and efficient, not the bloated and ponderous.

Remember: bigger size is not always better. Sometimes it is fatal.

Are there areas, such as overhead, facilities, staff, debt, or inventory, in which you should reduce costs now in order to increase profits later?

Every branch...that bears no fruit, he [God] takes away, and every branch that does bear fruit he prunes [trims], that it may bear [even] more fruit.
John 15:2 RSV

Dallas Wins Superbowl

Coach Tom Landry's Cowboys finally win the "big one" defeating Miami 24-3.

COACH TOM LANDRY

He was head coach of the Dallas Cowboys for 29 years and is a living legend. Probably more than any other person, he established the current image of the Cowboys as "America's Team."

After speaking together in El Paso, Tom and I rode in the limo to the airport. I was determined to learn more from this giant among coaches.

That day Tom reiterated what he believes are...

THREE DISTINCT KEYS TO CREATING A WINNING TEAM

1. CLEAR OBJECTIVE: "You must have a clear-cut, well-defined objective. Very few people really know what they want."

2. PLAN OF ACTION: "You must develop a plan of action that will enable you to accomplish your objective."

3. RECOGNIZE RESISTANCE: "You must realize that there will be forces of resistance released against your action plan to keep you from accomplishing your objective."[1]

In teaching about resistant forces, Tom goes beyond the normally taught strategies of setting goals, staying motivated, and remaining positive. He believes that by identifying the forces of resistance, strategies can be developed to overcome these hindering powers.

TOM LANDRY'S KEYS TO WINNING

According to Tom, the secret to developing success strategies is knowledge. He says, "The first requirement of leadership is knowledge."[2] When he became defensive player-coach of the New York Giants, he was only 29 years old. He couldn't establish his authority based on age or experience. Also, others had more athletic talent and football skill. What he did have was knowledge.

Tom would spend countless hours learning about opposing players and teams. He devoured anything and everything he could find concerning football.

He says, "All the hours of study that I had spent gave me an understanding of other teams' offenses. This knowledge of their offenses prepared and qualified me to lead the defense. The ability to convey that knowledge to my teammates earned me the respect required to lead effectively.

He says, "A leader doesn't have to be the smartest member of a group, but he does need to demonstrate a mastery of his field. Mastery means more than just knowing data and facts; it requires an understanding of the information and the ability to apply that information to the situation at hand."

Famous industrialist Andrew Carnegie struck the same chord when he said, "The number one weakness of most sales people is not knowing everything possible about their products and/or customers."

Coach Landry emphasizes, "A successful leader must be innovative, one step ahead of the crowd. Knowledge, combined with proper preparation, enables one to be innovative and overcome opposition."

What are you doing to become the "knowledge master" of your field?

...people are destroyed for lack of knowledge....
Hosea 4:6

Try ordering a medium-sized drink at many coffeehouses these days. They will look at you as though you had just asked for a coke.

The Wall Street Journal reports that "medium size is disappearing." Instead of "small," items are now being referred to as "individual," "disposable," or "short."

At Starbucks Coffee, a large size is called a "grande" and a medium size is referred to as "tall."

In this age of increased image-consciousness, marketers are carefully labeling their products to reflect the desire of consumers to obtain more for their money.

But consumers are not the only ones desiring things to be above average. So are employers.

Lee Iacocca, former president of Chrysler Corporation, says, "The kind of people that I look for to fill top management spots are the eager beavers, people who try to do more that they are expected to do — they always reach."[1]

Best-selling author Og Mandino states, "The only certain means of success is to render more and better service than is expected."

Ford Motor Company founder Henry Ford said, "Giving good service in business is the greatest guarantee of success any person can have."[2]

In every area of life ever-increasing numbers of people are wanting more out of life and are thinking above average. So says...

JOHN MASON

He is a personal friend, advisor, and successful author who caught this emerging consumer trend when he decided to title his best-selling book *An Enemy Called Average*.

John believes that "God has placed within each one of us something that cries out to be above average and extraordinary."[3]

Here are some of John Mason's treasures for...

DEFEATING AN ENEMY CALLED AVERAGE[4]

- "Don't ever start your day in neutral."
- "The more you look back the less you can see ahead."
- "Nothing dies quicker than a new idea in a closed mind."
- "The best time of the day is now."
- "You can't get ahead when you're trying to get even."
- "Success: getting up one more time than you fall down."
- "Let go of whatever makes you stop."
- "The key to your future is hidden in your daily approach to life."
- "Watch for big problems, they disguise big opportunities."
- "What you set your heart on will determine how you spend your life."
- "Find the problems you're an answer to."

What are you actively doing to raise yourself to a higher level of excellence and achievement? Who is creating your world?

Whatsoever thy hand findeth to do, do it with [all] thy might....
Ecclesiastes 9:10

Smart Money Won't Jingle

If a new form of electronic money becomes popular, people's frustrating search for change to plop in vending machines might be only a memory. Banks are now developing wallet-sized plastic cards that store small amounts of money as a substitute for pocket change.

Reading this article about not having change for vending machines reminded me of an interesting story I came across. It is about an event that happened to a college vice president in South Carolina.

One night, after settling in his motel room, the executive walked down the corridor to where the vending machines were located. He stood looking at the candy machine trying to decide which item to select.

Just then a ten-year-old boy walked up beside him and began to poke quarters into the machine. The boy dropped in three, four, six, eight, ten quarters.

Finally, the executive tapped the boy on the shoulder and said, "Son, you're putting way too much money in that machine."

The boy turned to him and proudly said, "Oh no sir. See, the more money I put in, the more stuff I get out."

A POWERFUL INCREASE PRINCIPLE

This little boy identified one of the key reasons why many achievers are not experiencing increase in certain areas of their lives. They are not making big enough deposits.

My spiritual life took on new power and vibrancy when I began to increase my spiritual deposits, scheduling regular times of Bible reading, praying, and listening to Scripture-based teaching tapes.

In the physical arena I began to experience increased alertness, better stamina, and improved health when I made the decision to increase my deposits of time in exercising and swimming.

Even in the financial arena, I have discovered a direct relationship between increased donations to my church and charities and the receiving of unexpected blessings and unusual business deals.

The closeness that my wife and I enjoy with our children and grandchildren is the result of the liberal deposits of time, attention, travel, spiritual enrichment, and money that we faithfully deposit into their lives.

If you are standing next to the "vending machine of life" wondering why you are not receiving a greater quantity of health, happiness, spiritual endowment, and/or financial rewards, I would suggest that you ask yourself, "What is the ratio of my actual deposits to my desired withdrawals?"

MAKE YOUR OWN HEADLINE

In what areas of your life would an increase in deposits of time, prayer, and/or money result in positive benefits or increase?

He who sows generously will reap a generous harvest.
2 Corinthians 9:6 MOFFATT

Snake's Skin Can't Grow

In order to grow bigger, snakes must shed their old skin and grow new outer skin because their skin doesn't expand and get bigger.

People are like snakes in that both shed their skins. However, with humans it is a continuous process over time, and the skin expands and grows bigger as the person does.

Snakes, on the other hand, are held captive by their skin. In order to grow larger, they must shed this outer barrier. However, people are held captive by their inner "skin" — their self-image.

Most people accept what experts refer to as an "inherited self-image." This is the image of self that results from the influence of environment, personal experiences, family and friends.

Achievers recognize that in order for their outer world to grow larger in size and/or influence, first their inner image must increase. Instead of accepting the image of what they are, they consciously create the image of what they desire to become. They grow internally in order to increase externally.

Dr. Maxwell Maltz, best-selling author of *Psychocybernetics*, reinforced this thought process when he declared, "People act like the person they conceive themselves to be."[1]

Zig Ziglar reiterates this same message: "A person cannot consistently perform in a manner which is inconsistent with the way they see themselves."[2]

Throughout the Bible, whenever God desired to use someone in a position of great leadership, He first dealt with any self-image problem that individual might have had.

As an example, when God called Moses to lead the Children of Israel out of Egypt, his inferior self-image immediately manifested. He replied, "Who am I? They will not believe me. I am slow of speech." God solved Moses' self-image problem by answering, "I AM is with thee," by empowering his rod, and by giving him an assistant and spokesman, his brother Aaron. (See Exodus 3 and 4.)

DENIS WAITLEY

One of my fellow success spokesmen, Denis Waitley and I recently shared the stage in Memphis teaching 30,000 people at a convention.

Denis stated, "What separates the winners from the losers in life, perhaps more than anything else, is self-esteem: That deep-down, inside-the-skin feeling of one's worth."

Denis believes that, almost without exception, the real winner, whether in sports, business, or any other activity of life, is the person who has a positive, increasing self-image.

Here are some of his image builders that I have learned.

DENIS WAITLEY'S SELF-IMAGE BUILDERS

1. TAKE INVENTORY: Write down what you have done so far in life that you are proud of, big and little.

2. MAKE A LIST: List on paper your best qualities and strengths. Also list positive alternatives to those negative habits you seriously want to change.

3. IMPROVE YOUR SKILLS: Maintain an ongoing self-improvement program emphasizing the positive improvements in your life that will result from change.

4. USE POSITIVE WORDS: Use encouraging, affirmative language when talking to yourself and to others about yourself. Focus on using uplifting and constructive adjectives and adverbs.

5. SET YOUR OWN INTERNAL STANDARDS: Don't compare yourself to others. You are unique. Measure yourself by your standards, not others'.

I would personally add to those items listed above: Remember that the God of Moses is still saying, "I AM is with thee." Let the realization that God will never leave you nor forsake you (Hebrews 13:5) empower your life and release fresh confidence to your being.

Like the snake, you are not captive to the old skin of self-image. You can grow internally, leave your current skin behind, and enjoy increase in any area of your life.

MAKE YOUR OWN HEADLINE

What can you do this month to improve your self-image? How might making a list of your strengths and best qualities affect your self-image?

"...I will be with thee...."
Exodus 3:12

A woman who died while going to a hearing to fight her job dismissal has been reinstated to her job. Authorities say the woman, who was revived by paramedics, has fully recovered.

When the last child at home moves out, gets married, or goes off to college, many parents believe their job of nurturing and mentoring has ended. For many, it seems as if they have been fired from a job that has consumed most of their time for most of their lives. However, many of these parents are discovering a new and exciting role — grandparenting.

Former president George Bush is one of those people. "One of my most important accomplishments is to be a huge success in the grandparent business."[1]

Another person achieving in this arena is...

ARVELLA SCHULLER

She is the wife of Dr. Robert Schuller of the Crystal Cathedral. She produces the "Hour of Power" television program, handles all the family's personal finances, has a speaking career, and does volunteer work.

However, despite her busy schedule and time pressures, Arvella's fifteen grandchildren are a top priority for her. She schedules time to give undivided attention to each one. If a grandchild has a special need, Arvella will be there regardless of her busy schedule.[2]

I came across the following poem which shows the conflicting viewpoints as to the role of a grandmother.

THE GRANDMOTHER POEM

In the dim and distant past,
When life's tempo wasn't as fast,
Grandma used to rock and knit,
Crochet, chat and baby-sit.
When the kids were in a jam,
They could always count on Gram.
In an age of gracious living,
Grandma was the gal for giving.

Now Grandma is at the gym,
Exercising to keep slim.
She's off touring with the bunch,
Or taking clients out to lunch.
Flying off to ski or curl,
All her days are in a whirl.
Nothing seems to shock her,
It seems that Grandma's off her rocker.

— Unknown

Arvella believes that the core issues of life do not require a grandparent to advocate his or her traditional role. She says, "In a time of changing roles certain roles need to remain unchanged."[3]

One of the most valuable things that a grandparent can do is to release his or her love, knowledge, wisdom, experience, and prayers into the lives of the younger generation.

MAKE YOUR OWN HEADLINE

How can you adjust your priorities or schedule in order to better mentor and influence your grandchildren or others of the younger generation? What are you doing now?

[Teach] the aged women likewise....that they may teach the young women to be sober, to love their husbands, to love their children.
Titus 2:3,4

Incredible stress that smothers creativity and brings feelings of anxiety and loss of control can be caused by trash pile up. It is possible to use up more energy in dealing with piles of mail, memos, and periodicals than in nurturing people and a business.

For example, one person's office was in such bad shape that a security officer reported to police that burglars had ransacked the place. Actually, it was how the office normally looked.

Professional organizers say the key to eliminating paper messes is to develop a personalized system, one that works and makes sense for the individual. Such a system must be based on the principle that everything needs to have a place, wherever that may be.

If disorganization is causing you to have trouble finding needed documents or computer files, or if someone else couldn't find them if you were absent, here are some helpful tips for establishing...

"Small efforts can add up to create giant results."
— Anthony Robbins

AN AUTOMATED TRASH SYSTEM

1. THROW IT AWAY (OR RECYCLE IT): Much of what you receive is useless, not applicable, or no longer timely. The quicker these items are removed the better.

2. ACT ON IT: If it is important and you must personally take care of it, get it done as quickly as possible. Create a "hot folder" for urgent matters.

3. REFER IT TO SOMEONE: If it is important but can be handled by someone else, forward it to that person.

4. SAVE IT/FILE IT: For items that must be used or referred to in the future, develop an easy to use "retrieval system" to assist with future discovery.

5. HALT IT: The less you receive, the less you have to deal with. Either reduce mail and subscriptions or have subordinates sift through them and only forward important articles and mail to you.

The main concept behind this "automated trash system" is to avoid throwing incoming papers in a pile to be dealt with later. Activating the above system will free you to new levels of creativity and productivity while increasing your desk space.

It may not seem like much, but as Anthony Robbins says, "Small efforts can add up to giant results."

MAKE YOUR OWN HEADLINE

What steps can you take to reduce the amount of paperwork you handle regularly? What systems can you create for better paper flow management?

Seest thou a man diligent in his business? he shall stand before kings....
Proverbs 22:29

The concept of making things happen is vital for anyone who desires to get ahead in life.

Achievers know that when circumstances demand, they must take control of the situation, break through the barriers of resistance, and seize an opportunity.

Many instances of this "make things happen" characteristic can be found in the Bible. The woman with the issue of blood pressed through the crowd to touch Jesus' garment, and was cured of her disease. (Matthew 9:18-22.) Four men removed the roof of a crowded house so their friend could be touched and healed by Jesus. (Mark 2:1-12.)

ROBERT TOWNSEND

I heard a good example of this decisive attitude at one of our seminars. It was shared by Jim Money, former head of Snelling and Snelling Personnel International. The story was about Robert Townsend, who

"I teach my
people to make
things happen."
— Roger Penske

was senior vice-president of American Express before becoming president of Avis Rent-A-Car.

MAKING THINGS HAPPEN

Several years ago a controller told Townsend that he thought he could make AMEX an extra $800,000 a day, but he needed a special computer to calculate whether his plan could actually work.

Townsend told the controller, "Get one now."

The controller replied, "If I turn in a requisition for one, it will take days, maybe weeks."

"I'll get you one," Townsend answered. He promptly went to their supplier and found one in stock. However, the supply manager would not release it to him without a formal requisition.

"I've got something better than a requisition," Townsend stated. "Sign this."

"What is it?" the supply manager asked.

"It's my letter of resignation," explained Townsend. "I want you to sign it so that when I deliver this to the president of the company and tell him that I am resigning because a senior vice president of AMEX can't get a computer from a supplier, he will know who you are."

He got his computer, and the controller used it to make American Express an extra $800,000 a day.

Television commentator Joe Gibbs, who is the former head coach of the Washington Redskins, believes that this ability to overcome negative circumstances and adversity is one of the keys to effective leadership. He says, "Don't think of trouble as a negative, but seize it as an opportunity to lap the field."[1]

Determine that you are going to be an overcomer. You won't have to battle alone. In the words of the late Norman Vincent Peale, "God is often most active when the darkness seems deepest."[2]

MAKE YOUR OWN HEADLINE

Have you empowered yourself, and your key people, to make the decisions necessary to seize profit opportunities?

Be strong, of good courage that you may succeed wherever you go.
Joshua 1:7 MOFFATT

Movie Star Makes Deathbed Confessions

The 67-year-old actor, who died in the arms of his fourth wife, was racked with shame and guilt as he apologized for the way he'd lived his life. It was reported he was deeply hurt that his three children from previous marriages refused to visit him on his deathbed.

St. Augustine once said that adulthood begins when a person asks himself the question, "What do I want to be remembered for?"

Former president George Bush has determined the answer to that question. He says, "I would like to be remembered for integrity, service, and family."[1]

It is good to be remembered for career accomplishments, personal achievements, financial success, or noble efforts on behalf of the less fortunate. However, I believe that one of the most important things to be remembered for is a life marked by exemplary character. This kind of life becomes a role model for others, especially one's own children.

Such a life was lived by my father...

DR. IRVINE HARRISON

Besides being immensely successful, having earned two doctor's degrees, and enjoying achievements in many different arenas, my father also lived a life based upon principle. He did not just read the Bible, he lived it. He was a decisive leader who had the ability to persevere and win, but he was also a man of love, forgiveness, and integrity. I never saw him cheat or heard him lie.

As I stood behind the casket at his funeral to address the hundreds gathered there, I was so grateful to be the son of a man of such positive character.

WHAT DO I TELL YOU WHEN DAD IS GONE?

Do I tell you about my feelings for my father?

That I loved and respected him, that I will miss him?

Do I tell you about his life of character and integrity?

That I never heard him tell a lie nor saw him cheat anyone?

Do I tell you about our great family experiences?

How he invested in his children by including them in many trips and outings?

Do I tell you about his concern for his son's future?

How he gave caring advice and financial support?

No. All the above is true, but the most important thing I can tell you about dad is the "faith of my father."

He lived his life to please God and to help others find the reality of a relationship with Jesus Christ.

My dad died on my 29th birthday. For my present that year, I received a memory of a man of character, a man who loved his family, had faith in God, and daily lived the Christian life. This memory has inspired and directed me throughout my life.

> **Power Point**
>
> "No one on their deathbed says, 'I should have spent more time at the office.'"
> — Barbara Walters

What are the most important characteristics you would like to be remembered for? What are you doing to develop these traits?

...he had this testimony [memory], that he pleased God.
Hebrews 11:5

Thieves Steal Family History

A lifetime of pictures and videos of the family were among some of the items taken from a couple's station wagon as it sat in their driveway. The pictures, which were the only ones of their children growing up, were packed in the vehicle for a trip the next morning to a family reunion.

Can you handle a major loss of important personal documents or business records?

Every day disasters — whether man-induced or natural — unexpectedly blast businesses and homes of all kinds and sizes in America. Some recover quickly. Others never do.

A recent University of Texas study of companies which had suffered catastrophic data losses showed that nearly 50 percent polled were never able to reopen. Worse yet, two years later, 94 percent of the companies had not been able to survive the resulting calamity.

Whether on a corporate or a personal basis, achievers must focus on protecting their valuable keepsakes and proprietary resources.

This is not to encourage the adoption of a mentality of expecting the worst. However, it is always best to be aware of possible negative occurrences in order to develop prevention strategies and/or minimize their negative impact. Catastrophic events may be harmful, but they need not be disastrous.

"What you do not value and protect you will probably lose."
— Bob Harrison

Here are some suggestions on...

HOW TO BE DISASTER-RESISTANT

1. MAKE A COPY: Keep a backup of important documents and computer files stored in a safe place off premises.

2. PROTECT FROM FIRE: Store important legal documents or working papers in fireproof cabinets on premises.

3. LOCK IT UP: Keep confidential material double locked — locked files in a locked office. Require distinct individual security codes for office entry after hours.

4. DON'T TELL OTHERS WHAT YOU HAVE: Require all employees to sign proprietary rights statements protecting the confidentiality and secrecy of customers and their file information.

5. ESTABLISH A RECYCLE POLICY: Do not release new confidential information without the old information having being returned — and destroyed.

6. KEEP IT CONFIDENTIAL: Place shredding machines in the offices where confidential reports and documents are discarded. Most trash is public domain once it leaves the premises.

Without a prevention and recovery plan, you may face the biggest disaster of all — losing business.

MAKE YOUR OWN HEADLINE

Have you adequately protected important documents, lists, records, assets, and pictures whose value is so great that replacing them would be impossible or extremely costly?

...the substance of a diligent man is precious.
Proverbs 12:27

North Carolina Basketball Coach Dean Smith passes the late Adolph Rupp at Kentucky as the NCAA's winningest coach of all time.

They came from near and far to watch and cheer for him. Minutes after winning his 877th game — breaking the record as the winningest basketball coach in NCAA history — Dean Smith was mobbed by fans, former players, and reporters.

To his family — and those who know him — he has achieved just as much away from basketball as on the court. What are some of the success secrets that have enabled this man of character and courage to rise to the top of his profession and be so respected?

1. INNOVATIVENESS — Rival coaches say his innovations have made his teams tough to prepare for — and beat. Matching wits with Dean Smith over the years often has been like solving basketball's version of a differential equation. From the four-corners offense to zone traps to Smith's famous "blue team" of five players coming off the bench at one time, he specializes in the unexpected.

2. MAXIMUM THINKING — He creates an environment whereby his players are willing to make that extra effort and do the things necessary to be strong every year.

3. COMPETITIVE SPIRIT — He strives for success. Duke coach Mike Krzyzewski says... "You better not miss a step or he'll hold you accountable for it."

4. CONSISTENCY — He's been winning big, at the same school, for nearly forty years. He doesn't change moods. He has developed the unique ability to keep the intensity and adrenaline flowing year after year.

5. COURAGE — He is a man of principle. During the 1960's, he was instrumental in helping integrate in the university and community.

6. PREPARATION — His teams are always well-prepared. He's the son of two teachers and puts that background to good use. Former Virginia coach Terry Holland says, "I found that practices leading up to a North Carolina game were very difficult and it often took days of preparation to be at our best against them."

7. CARING ATTITUDE — He is more than a coach to the players; he is their friend. He is just as concerned about the 13th guy on the team as he is about the stars. Smith knows his players' interests, dreams, dates of special occasions, hobbies, and relatives. The coach stays in contact and helps them even after graduation.

If you desire to "Leap into History" by reaching the upper levels of success in your chosen profession or with significant contributions to others, then the above characteristics should be a part of your life's game plan.

MAKE YOUR OWN HEADLINE

Which of the above characteristics do you need most to improve in? What can you do to begin this process?

_____

"Seest thou a man diligent in his business?
He shall stand before kings."
Proverbs 22:29

_____

Race Driver Goes Clean

Stock car driver Darrell Waltrip announced the changing of his race car team sponsorship. He dropped a beer company and signed up with a laundry detergent company as a new sponsor.

P eople live their lives according to their own self-image and the image others hold of them. One man who knows about image is stock car driver...

DARRELL WALTRIP

I came across a short story about Waltrip changing sponsorship and, more importantly, why he decided to do so.

Shortly after he miraculously survived a Daytona 500 crash, he began attending church with his wife. A new joy and purpose entered his life.

One day as he and his wife were visiting with their pastor, the minister asked, "I notice that your car is sponsored by a beer company. Is that the image you want to portray of yourself?"

The issue was not beer drinking. It was the kind of image that this type of sponsorship would create for him.

Darrell thought about it. He did care about his image. He thought, "If our prayers for a child are answered, what kind of dad do I want to be? What kind of image do I want my son or daughter to have of me?"[1]

An opportunity opened for him to sign with a new racing team sponsored by a laundry detergent company! Remembering his pastor's admonition to walk the walk, not just talk the talk, he decided to switch teams.

Two years later, daughter Jessica was born, and a few years later, daughter Sarah. In 1989, Darrell won the premier race of the stock car circuit — the Daytona 500.

Waltrip changed sponsors when he got hold of the principle that our lives and our image replicate themselves in the lives of others. We must remember: we are an example to others, especially our own children.

LITTLE CHILDREN FOLLOW ME

A careful man I must be,
Little children follow me.
I do not dare go astray,
For they will go the self-same way.

I cannot escape their watchful eye,
Whatever they see me do, they'll try.
Like me they say they're going to be,
Little children who follow me.

I must remember as I go,
Through summer suns and winter snows,
As I am building, for the years to be,
That little children follow me.

— Unknown

Would you be willing for someone to videotape your personal life and then use that tape as a training device for others?

"It were better for him that a millstone were hanged about his neck, and he cast into the sea, than that he should offend one of these little ones."
Luke 17:2

Saboteurs Derail Train

Saboteurs pulled 29 spikes from a stretch of railroad track, sending an Amtrak train hurtling off a bridge into a dry creek bed. Cars plunged from the bridge at 50 mph with three of them coming to rest lying on their sides on the sandy bottom of a desert wash.

One of the biggest challenges facing achievers is that of staying on track and avoiding personal and professional derailment.

Most success-oriented people are proficient at setting goals, motivating themselves, creating teams, handling financial challenges, and generating enthusiasm. However, while learning to master these skills and racing along the track to success, tragically, many of them are unexpectedly derailed. They find themselves — or their companies — "derailed on the sandy bottom of a desert wash."

Here are some strategies for...

STAYING ON TRACK

1. WATCH THE DETAILS: The removal of a few rail spikes can derail an entire train. Are you regularly checking and inspecting the small but important areas of your life?

2. STAY GOAL-FOCUSED: Momentum is achieved, not in the switchyard of multiple choices, but on a single track heading toward a predetermined destination.

3. MAINTAIN CHARACTER: Don't just stay on track financially. Live a morally consistent life. Private victories lead to a life of public impact and influence.

4. BALANCE PRIORITIES: If a train gets too off balance, it will overturn. So will you. Give time and attention to all the important areas of your life: marital, familial, personal, professional, physical, and spiritual.

5. MAINTAIN PROPER FUEL LEVELS: Enthusiasm is an incredible fuel. However, there is a fuel additive that will infuse your life with new power. It is the presence of the Holy Spirit. This presence is a result of time spent reading the Bible, praising and worshipping God, and engaging in personal meditation. Also, the Holy Spirit can warn you of impending dangers and empower you to climb the mountains that lie ahead on the track to greatness.

The desired outcome of a goal-oriented life is to arrive at the desired destination as quickly and efficiently as possible. Stay on track by implementing the above strategies.

MAKE YOUR OWN HEADLINE

What are you doing to prevent personal and professional "derailment"? Can you list situations that are possible goal derailers?

"...turn not from it [God's will] to the right hand or to the left, that thou mayest prosper withersoever thou goest."
Joshua 1:7

Hawaii Rebuilds Tourism

By emphasizing the Hawaiian culture, the islands' resorts are rebuilding their tourism, which nose-dived in the early 1990's. Many believe the Hawaii Tourism Department made a mistake when it started marketing itself as another "fun and sun" destination, rather than playing up Hawaii's unique cultural identity.

A Gallup Poll of 250,000 successful people found that "the highest levels of personal achievement came when people matched their activities with their strengths."

It is evident that every company, city, state, product, or book possesses unique strengths — characteristics — that distinguish it from all others.

The same is true for people. Each of us has abilities, talents, skills, knowledge, connections, and experiences that distinguish us from others. I call these unique characteristics "armor."

A company will always do better — and make more money — by focusing on its proven armor and that of each member of its team.

NBA coach Pat Riley says, "Every member of a team plays a different role and brings different skills."[1]

A good Biblical example is found in the story of David, the shepherd boy.

David was able to defeat the giant, Goliath, only because he fought the battle using his strengths. The Bible states that when David was given the king's sword and armor he refused to fight with them because he had not proven them. (1 Samuel 17:38,39.)

David was an expert with the slingshot and was victorious in battle only because he used his proven armor, his unique strengths — stones and a slingshot. (Verses 40-50.)

DEMOS SHAKARIAN

Just as God used a shepherd boy to defeat a giant, He was able to use an Armenian farmer from California to launch one of the most powerful Christian businessmen's organizations of all time. The Full Gospel Business Men's Fellowship International was made possible because a man named Demos Shakarian understood this principle of "using your armor," as revealed in his book...

THE HAPPIEST PEOPLE ON EARTH

"If there is one thing I had learned over the...years,...it was that...each individual had his special function. Some men were born organizers. Some were anointed speakers. Others could counsel. And when anyone assumed a function that wasn't his, he not only did a second-rate job, he blocked the flow of power to the person it did belong to.

"As for me....I was a *helper*. My gift was to provide a place and a time and a way for other men to shine. It wasn't a lesser gift than anyone else's, or a greater. It was simply mine."[2]

My friend Peter Lowe, who is known as America's Premier Success Seminar Organizer, believes that the concept of recognizing his armor is one of his success secrets. He says, "Don't keep reinventing yourself. Discover what you are to do and then stick with it. You may change your tactics and methods, but stay with your core principles and calling."

Career experts estimate that at least half of those working are not in jobs suited to their primary interests and abilities.[3]

It is important for you to identify your strengths and gifts, particularly in the work arena so that your passion and energy are allowed to be released.

What are your unique gifts and callings? What are the different strengths of your team? What are you doing to maximize their use?

...David said..., "I cannot go with these; for I have not proved them...."
1 Samuel 17:39

An achiever's life is much like that of an air traffic controller: It is spent in guiding people and projects to designated destinations.

As with a controller, an achiever's ability to communicate effectively is a must, or great turmoil and confusion will result. It is not enough just to communicate, however. There must be an assurance that the message has been received and that it has been implanted upon the memory of the receiver.

I came across a story that demonstrates the chaos and financial loss that can occur when this important communication cycle is incomplete.

CECIL B. DEMILLE

Cecil B. DeMille was one of Hollywood's all-time great movie film makers, creating such cinematic masterpieces as *The Ten Commandments*. However, even he was not immune to foul ups, as in the case of the expensive communication problem that occurred while he was filming an epic battle scene in another Biblical film.

Power Point

"Achievers
have systems
to verify that
messages
have been
received and
understood."
— Bob Harrison

The large cast had begun rehearsing at 6:00 A.M. During the long day, they had practiced the extravagant battle scene four times.

Now the sun was setting, and there was just enough time before dark to shoot the actual sequence. Eleven cameras had been strategically placed to record every aspect of the scene, including some which had been carefully situated to catch the stars in close-ups as they engaged in "hand-to-hand combat."

DeMille looked over the panorama and gave the command, "Action!"

Hundreds of costumed extras charged the hill to do mock battle, while actors dressed as Roman centurions whipped at two hundred "slaves," who were supposed to be moving a huge stone monument.

When the fifteen-minute battle sequence was over, enormously pleased, DeMille turned and waved to the camera crew supervisor perched on a nearby hilltop. The supervisor waved back, raised his megaphone, and yelled to DeMille, "Ready to film when you are!"

He had missed the command, "Action!" Presuming the crew was still practicing, he had not filmed any of the scene!

Oftentimes in the real world, botched "scenes" cannot be "reshot," and opportunities may be lost forever. To avoid costly foul ups, be sure that your important communications have all three key elements: "Message sent, message received, and message understood."

MAKE YOUR OWN HEADLINE

Do you have an adequate system for "feedback acknowledgment" of important messages?

They have ears, but they hear not....
Psalm 135:17

The Bomb Is In The Mail

Mysterious bomber strikes again.
Package explodes in executive's office.

The bomb is in the male. It is also in some females. The bomb referred to here in this context is the time bomb of fatigue, ticking away toward a violent outburst of anger, or counting down to total exhaustion.

Bill Hybels, noted pastor and seminar speaker from the Chicago area, says, "Not only are physically run-down people short on energy, but they tend to be easily irritated, critical, defensive, and negative. It is hard for them to love others, and it is equally hard for others to love them."

Best-selling author and personal friend Richard Exley says, "Don't deceive yourself. Rest is not optional....In Old Testament times, Sabbath-breakers were executed."[1]

Real estate mogul Donald Trump says, "To be successful, it is not enough to have brains; you must have the energy."

In her book *Jesus-Led*, Laurie Beth Jones states, "Leaders must be aware that their energy is subject to depletion and they must make guarding that energy reserve a priority."[2]

T. D. Jakes

Bishop T.D. Jakes sums up the dangers of fatigue in his best-selling book, *Loose That Man and Let Him Go.*

Fatigue: The Silent Cancer

"Fatigue is the silent cancer of people's judgment and emotions. It robs them of creativity and secretly steals their energy and discernment. Tired people are more vulnerable and less careful. Even simple problems seem insurmountable. When fatigue robs people of their better judgment, they make permanent decisions based on the stress of temporary circumstances. Oftentimes these people are hard to work for and hard to love. They are not led, but rather are driven...to total exhaustion!

"The Bible teaches that even the soil becomes depleted if it tries to produce without a season of rest. There is a time and a season for all things. (Ecclesiastes 3:1.)

"Success is their addiction and affliction. A normal night's sleep can no more cure their exhaustion than a Band-Aid can cure invasive cancer.

"These people need rest...not only physical rest...but the rest that comes from placing their lives in the will of God. Take time to rest and renew...and bring balance to your life."[3]

Make Your Own Headline

Are you physically or emotionally exhausted? What can you do to break this cycle and empower yourself?

There remaineth therefore a rest to the people of God.
Hebrews 4:9

Earl Nightengale struck the same chord as Tom Hopkins, a premiere sales trainer and best-selling author, when he stated, "People who begin by setting goals (the determining of desired destinations) succeed because they know where they are going."

To achieve success you must know where you are going.

Many people are riding on the merry-go-round of life. They are moving and changing horses but are not going anywhere.

Jesus knew where He was going and what His purpose was. His whole life was focused on an end goal — death on the cross and resurrection to new and eternal life.

Best-selling author Stephen Covey refers to this goal-oriented mindset as Success Habit #2. He calls it "beginning with the end in mind," referring to the strategy of never beginning anything before determining the desired end result.[1] This involves making both the beginning and the ending memorable and significant.

MAXIMIZE THE BEGINNING AND ENDING

"You can't get
to a place you
have never
been without
knowing where
you are going."
— Tom Hopkins

I first became aware of the importance of this concept at the age of 17, well before Covey's book was written. I had won the competition to lead my high school marching band in its football half-time shows. I was also given the responsibility of creating each show theme and then teaching the band the formations needed in preparation for the presentation.

During the preceding summer, I attended drum major training school. The headmaster stated, "The secret to success with a half-time show is its beginning and ending. Make sure these two elements are done well, and you'll do okay."

During the football season, I concentrated on those two elements, and the band received rave reviews and wild enthusiasm about our performances.

From that time on, I have endeavored to have a good beginning and ending in everything I do — whether it is delivering a speech, going on a family outing, or even following my daily routine.

If you are not already implementing this kind of end-in-mind increase thinking as a regular part of daily routine, then begin now. Your life will take on a new dimension of power, and you will not end up wasting time going down a road to nowhere.

MAKE YOUR OWN HEADLINE

Do you believe a person can lead without knowing where he or she is going? Have you clearly defined your personal or professional mission? Have you clearly communicated to others involved the desired end result of all your planned projects and goals?

...Jesus answered...."To this end was I born...."
John 18:37

A chievers don't just believe that it's right to work, they love to work. They do not see work as a negative necessity, but as a positive process that results in fulfillment and increase.

Robert Schuller says that triumph is made up of two words — "try" and "umph."

Margaret Thatcher, former prime minister of Great Britain, says, "I do not know anyone who has got...to the top without hard work. That is the recipe."[1]

Jesus taught about the work ethic in the parable of the three servants. (Matthew 25:14-30.) A landlord gave each of his servants money to oversee while he was gone. When he returned, he inquired how each had handled his funds. Jesus referred to the two who had worked and doubled the money as "good and faithful." The one who did not have a work ethic and did nothing, He referred to as "wicked and slothful."

A good example of a person with a strong work ethic was...

The late Dr. Sumrall was president and founder of Feed the Hungry, a multi-million-dollar relief organization. Until his recent death, even though he was in his 80's, he flew over 200,000 miles a year speaking and overseeing food distribution efforts, operated a television and radio empire, and authored several new books every year.

A study of his childhood reveals this work trait mentality.

"PEANUTS AND A BLOCK OF ICE"

"As a little boy, I would go down to the local wholesale house and buy hundred-pound bags of peanuts. I would take them home, bake them in the oven, and put them into small bags. I then went to the lumber mill and sold them to the men who worked there.

"In addition, during the summer I also went into the snowball business. I built myself a wagon from scraps and covered it with canvas. I pulled the wagon over to the ice house and bought a block of ice. I then collected different flavors of syrup, an ice scraper, and paper cups and sold ice snowballs. I normally cleared a good profit."[3]

Along with character and a positive attitude, a strong work ethic is one of the most important natural ingredients for an achiever to possess — and look for when interviewing prospective employees.

Remember, the only place that increase comes before work is in the dictionary!

MAKE YOUR OWN HEADLINE

What can you do to increase your personal work desire and ethic and that of your subordinates?

...the people had a mind to work.
Nehemiah 4:6

House Expands Quality Jobs Act

The state legislature passed a bill which expands tax incentives to major new and growing businesses.

In today's competitive marketplace, if you desire your business to expand and experience growth, then your management focus must include an emphasis on quality.

"Not every product is sold on the basis of quality, but if yours is and your quality starts to slip, you're dead." So says best-selling author Harvey Mackay.[1]

When Ritz-Carlton Hotels won the Malcolm-Baldridge Quality Award as one of the best-run businesses in the country, its president said that the key was the company's commitment to what he called "Total Quality."

He went on to define this term as "redesigning products and services so that customers get what they want and if those needs change, having a system in place that informs you quickly, so that you can design new products and services to satisfy them."[2]

On a recent TV special Stanley Marcus, the founder of Neiman Marcus department stores, was discussing his secrets of success. One in particular he emphasized was the old adage, "Quality will be remembered long after the price is forgotten."

Joe Griffith says, "Good quality is cheap; it's poor quality that is expensive."[3]

Tom Peters teaches that the secret to attaining good quality is measurement: "What gets measured (inspected) gets done. Measurement is the heart of any quality improvement process."[4]

The Japanese car maker, Toyota, increased its market share (and profits) in America in the early 1990's with a quality measurement program titled "Rapid Inch-Up." It was based upon the concept that if you make enough tiny steps, pretty soon you will outdistance the competition.

A decision for quality should not be relegated to the business arena alone, but should be applied to our personal lives as well.

The late Martin Luther King, Jr., exclaimed, "The quality, not the longevity of one's life is what is important."[5]

Probably no modern-day company has made better use of a commitment to quality than...

STARBUCKS COFFEE

In a short span of time Starbucks has skyrocketed from a six-store company in Seattle to an 800-store empire serving as a refuge to more than three million coffee drinkers each week and enjoying multi-million-dollar annual commercial sales.

CAFE LATTE AND CAPPUCCINO

"You can make the greatest coffee bad, but you can't make bad coffee good," says CEO Howard Schultz.

"We noticed that the majority of products on the market today focus on a baseline of mediocrity. Companies are looking for ways to conserve expenses to make more money. The easiest thing to do is say, 'Let's just cut the cost by two or three percent.' We've always done the reverse. We've looked for ways to improve quality by three or four percent.

"Our buyers work closely with the growers to assure quality so we can offer the world's best coffee.

"We are so fanatical about quality that all coffee is tracked from the time it comes into the store. Since coffee is fresh for only seven days on the shelf, on the eighth day it goes to charity. There's no fudging. We donated more coffee last year than most companies roast."

At Starbucks there is a passionate commitment to being the best.

MAKE YOUR OWN HEADLINE

Are you and/or your company passionately committed to the pursuit of quality and excellence? What steps can you take to increase quality? Why not start a personal quality "Rapid Inch-Up" process today?

And God saw every thing that he had made, and, behold,
it was very good....
Genesis 1:31

State Abolishes Slavery

Some 130 years after the Civil War ended, Mississippi voted to officially abolished slavery. In a symbolic move, the state senate endorsed the 13th Amendment to the U.S. Constitution.

Reading the above article brought to my memory an incredible woman who was at the forefront of breaking the barrier of racial discrimination in our nation — Rosa Parks.

The courage of this one lady was a force that helped empower a movement that caused this nation to change.

THE STRENGTH OF COURAGE

Achieving in any arena requires courage. The dictionary defines courage as "the ability to face danger or difficulties without fear."[1]

Mark Twain gave a little different interpretation: "Courage is resistance to fear, mastery of fear — not absence of fear."[2]

Ed Cole, author of *Maximized Manhood*, says, "Courage enables a person to encounter disapproval and contempt without departing from what is right. Success is not only based upon the ability to say yes, but to say no. Without courage, change will not take place. Without change, there can be no progress."[3]

THE QUIET STRENGTH OF ROSA PARKS

"I did not get on the bus to get arrested; I got on the bus to go home. Getting arrested was one of the worst days in my life. It was not a happy experience.

"On Thursday evening, December 1, I was riding the bus home from work. A white man got on, and the driver looked our way and said, 'Let me have those seats.' It did not seem proper to give my seat to a man.

"Three of the blacks in my row got up. I made up my mind not to move. I stayed in my seat and slid closer to the window. I do not remember being frightened. I have learned over the years that when one's mind is made up, this diminishes fear. I knew someone had to take the first step.

"I had no idea that history was being made. Our mistreatment was just not right, and I was tired of giving in. I felt the Lord would give me strength to endure whatever I had to face.

"The driver asked me if I was going to stand up and move. I answered, 'No. I am not.'"[4]

Her subsequent arrest for refusing to surrender a bus seat started the Montgomery bus boycott, catapulted Martin Luther King, Jr., to the national limelight, and helped bring an end to racial segregation in this country.

Harvey Mackay believes that most people meet fear when they take on true responsibility. Oftentimes this causes them to become less ambitious. He says, "What most people do not know is that courage can be learned."[5]

"To bring about the kind of change that causes the world to take notice, you must have courage."
— Rosa Parks

What can you do to increase your courage and overcome the fears that have been keeping you from achieving on a higher level?

Be strong and courageous, do not fear or be dismayed...
2 Chronicles 32:7 NASB

Airline Plans Expansion At Love Field

One of the nation's fastest growing airlines announced a seventy-two million dollar construction project at Love Field.

Do you need to expand your "Love Field"?

According to the late Norman Vincent Peale, "Positive love can restore energy, stimulate better health, and reinvigorate one's vitality."

Here are the steps recommended by Dr. Peale to become a more lovable person:

1. Focus on people's positive characteristics.

2. Deliberately eliminate ill will and hatred.

3. Pray for people by name.

4. Send positive love thoughts to people.

One individual who has followed all these steps to achieve personal and corporate success is my friend...

BRIAN GILLESPIE

Brian is vice-president of ITT Sheraton Reservations International and one of America's rising "super executives." What he has accomplished, before his 40th birthday, is awesome. One of his success secrets is based upon the principle of love and faithfulness.

LOVE AND FAITHFULNESS

When Brian left AT&T to work for ITT Sheraton, he joined a company that was so dissatisfied with its reservations group, it was secretly negotiating to sell it.

"The customers were not impressed. The owners were dissatisfied, and most of the employees were not happy and had a zero emotional bank account. They didn't trust the management, and they certainly didn't care about me," recalls Brian.

In order to change things, Brian realized that he had to convince his fellow workers that he viewed them as important fellow human beings — that he loved them, cared for them, and wanted the best for them. He could do so effectively because, being a Christian, God's love was in him to release.

At a gathering of leaders at my home one evening, Brian shared how he turned the situation around.

"We changed from skill-based and interaction training to 'whole person' training. Soon the employees began to feel secure, enjoyed working, were fulfilled in their jobs, absenteeism decreased, and productivity increased."

Several months later, ITT Sheraton conducted an employee satisfaction survey. Brian's group was number one. They had gone from being "worst in class" to the very best.

Zig Ziglar says, "People don't care how much you know, until they know how much you care — about them."

He continues, "Most anyone can do a job — but it's not until there is love in a person's heart for a job that the results will be great."[1]

The late Dale Carnegie taught about the astounding popularity of former president Theodore Roosevelt. He said, "Even his servants loved him."[2]

Jesus demonstrated that loving, caring attitude everywhere He went. He focused on helping and blessing others.

As you purpose to live this way, you will not only see productivity increase, but you will experience a more fulfilling and satisfying life.

MAKE YOUR OWN HEADLINE

What can you do to become a more loving and caring person?

Love and faithfulness keep a king safe; through love his throne is
made secure.
Proverbs 20:28 NIV

Globe Littered With Land Mines

It is now estimated that the world is littered with 80 million to 100 million anti-personnel land mines spread over 64 different countries. They may look harmless, but their ability to kill or maim is just a footstep away.

The road to increase is also littered with mines. The purpose of these mines is not to attack physically, but to destroy dreams and demolish creative ideas.

These mines are housed in the minds and hearts of those who oppose change. They normally are ignited and explode out of the mouths of their carriers when someone suggests that there is a better way, a different method, another viewpoint, or a need to change.

In order to succeed, you must be ready to walk through these mine fields of criticism, skepticism, ridicule, and unbelief.

Don't let others "blow up" your dreams. Remind yourself that on the other side of the mine fields of negative "can't-do-it" thinking are great rewards and significance.

Look at these words of opposition and anti-change attitude that history has recorded.

LAND MINES OF THE PAST

"Drill into the ground to try and find oil? You're crazy."

— Workers to Edwin L. Drake, 1859

"The 'telephone' has too many shortcomings to be seriously considered as a means of communication. The device is inherently of no value to us."

— Western Union executive memo, 1876

"Heavier-than-air flying machines are impossible."

— President, British Royal Society, 1895

"Who the hell wants to hear actors talk?"

— Major movie studio owner, 1927

"I have traveled the length and breadth of this country and talked with the best people, and I can assure you that data processing is a fad that won't last out the year."

— Major publisher's book editor, 1957

"Don't like their sound...guitar music is on the way out."

— Recording company executive, rejecting the Beatles, 1962

When the shepherd boy David volunteered to fight the giant Goliath in their epic battle, he encountered this "can't-do" opposition. Even his brother verbally attached him, saying, "...Why camest thou down hither? and with whom hast thou left those few sheep in the wilderness? I know thy pride, and the naughtiness [evil] of thine heart..." (1 Samuel 17:28).

In his book, *Peak Performance Principles for High Achievers*, John Noe states that the high achiever "...struggles against overwhelming obstacles and labors in the face of sharp criticism — but they have the heart to pursue when others quit."[1]

Power Point

"Great spirits will always encounter violent opposition from mediocre people."

— Albert Einstein

Determine afresh that you are not going to permit small-thinking, negative-oriented people to keep you from your destiny.

Are you letting other people's negative words and/or actions keep you from crossing your "field of dreams"?

So we see that they [the unfaithful Hebrews] could not enter in [to the Promised Land] because of unbelief.
Hebrews 3:19

Man Trapped In Outhouse Over Night

A man was rescued after spending a hot summer night trapped in an outhouse. According to authorities, he "was unhurt but in a pretty foul mood."

Don't let waste "stink up" your life — particularly time waste.

William Penn once said, "Time is what we want most, but what we use worst."

If you want to experience success, you must continually evaluate your daily routine to insure that you are performing the highest level of tasks and priorities. That is one of the real secrets of success for...

GEORGE SHINN

He is the owner of the NBA basketball team, the Charlotte Hornets, and operates some 30 other corporations. He believes that "time is a person's most precious commodity. Whatever your goals are, they must be accomplished in the time you have available. The way you occupy your time should be of paramount importance to you. With forethought and action, you can make your time pay high dividends, whether it is time spent at work or leisure."

"...since time is so valuable to us in achieving our goals, we should consider what robs us of productive time...."

— George Shinn

He believes that "...since time is so valuable to us in achieving our goals, we should consider what robs us of productive time...."[1]

From his book, *The Miracle of Motivation*, here are some of George's strategies on...

How To Eliminate Time Wasters

1. DISTRACTIONS AND INTERRUPTIONS: Some interruptions are unavoidable, but often they are caused by people just dropping in to chat. Protect yourself from these distractions.

2. THE LONG LUNCH HOUR: If you are trying to save time, beware! With travel and waiting time, a one-hour lunch appointment can easily use up two to three hours of your time. Explore alternatives.

3. PUTTING THINGS OFF: Oftentimes taking immediate action is better than pushing decisions off until a later day, even though it may result in extra work later.

4. COMMITTE MEETINGS: Few activities waste more time than meetings. Make sure they start on time, end on time, have a definite agenda, and everyone comes prepared.

5. WORRY: "Worry is one of the greatest time wasters." Faith and action will eliminate most worries.[2]

In the Bible, in the sixth chapter of the book of Acts, the apostles were faced with a time challenge. They couldn't wait on tables and still have time for ministry activities. They solved their time problem by delegating certain tasks to others so they themselves could focus on their highest calling.

You must learn to do the same.

Which time-wasting activities can you eliminate or drastically reduce?

...It would be a grave mistake for us...to wait at table.

Acts 6:2 NEB

City Makes U-Turns Legal

The Tulsa City Council did a turnabout on the ban of U-turns after surveying traffic laws in 15 other cities.

I love U-turns. The thought of being able to quickly change direction when needed or desired appeals to me. That is one reason why my all-time favorite football games involved massive U-turns of emotions, performance, and scores. Such as...

USC VS. NOTRE DAME — 1974

USC, which was facing the number-one ranked defense of the country, was behind 24-0. Just before half-time the game seemed hopeless. Then USC turned the game around by scoring 54 unanswered points and beating Notre Dame 54-24.

BUFFALO VS. HOUSTON — 1993 NFL PLAYOFFS

By the middle of the third quarter, Houston held a seemingly insurmountable 35-3 lead. Buffalo's second-string quarterback Frank Reich was brought into the game. He came off the bench and sparked the team back to an unbelievable 41-38 win. It was the biggest turnaround in NFL playoff history.

It Was Like A Horror Story

Another reason I identify with turnarounds, particularly in near impossible circumstances, is that I have been a part of several of them.

None of them was more personally meaningful than what happened to me at a Southern California Chrysler dealership.

I was a 30-year-old rookie with virtually no automotive sales experience. Because of my great success in the automobile leasing business, I was brought in as a last-ditch effort by the owners in an attempt to avoid bankruptcy and save the business.

It was out of money and losing more every day.

Customers were avoiding the place like the plague, the good sales people had fled, the inventory was grossly overstocked with gas-guzzling dinosaurs, and the gasoline crisis was in full bloom.

I was stuck with nearly 100 new gas guzzlers that no one was buying. I knew that I had to "dump" them regardless of profit, but how then could I cover the losses and continue in business?

I felt strongly that God had given me this opportunity so I knew that there had to be some hidden secret key to survival. Not knowing exactly what to, I went to prayer for direction and wisdom.

I remember that throughout the Bible people experienced miracle breakthroughs by using what they already had. With the starving woman, it was her last handful of meal. (1 Kings 17.) With the hungry multitude, it was the little lad's five loaves and two fishes. (Mark 6.)

Then the thought came to me: the secret to the survival of the business was the used car inventory. I could immediately purchase used four and six-cylinder cars from wholesalers and at the auction. These vehicles were popular and would make a profit.

Quickly, I began to load the lot with hot-selling used economy cars. I then started a massive new car liquidation sale. I sold them for anything reasonable — and some for a price that wasn't even reasonable. The used car profits offset the new car losses, so I was able to eliminate the problem of the overstocked new gas guzzlers.

This strategy successfully liquidated our new car inventory, took us through the crisis, and created sales momentum. This momentum attracted customers and new sales people. Soon the place was buzzing. Not only did the dealership survive, but within ninety days it had skyrocketed to the top ten of Chrysler/Plymouth stores in Southern California.

If you need to create a "U-turn" in some area of your life, ask yourself — and pray about — what change you can make in thinking, motivation, marketing, and/or action. Many times all you need is already there waiting to be discovered.

MAKE YOUR OWN HEADLINE

Where do you turn for help with tough decisions? What talents or goods do you now possess that could release increase?

...the Lord giveth wisdom....
Proverbs 2:6

Massive Flooding Leaves 21 Million Homeless

Disease and hunger ravaged the land as flood waters, which covered over 75 percent of the country, receded.

How should a person react to a tragedy such as the one described in this article, or help the hurting people encountered every day in the marketplace of life?

One person who discovered the answer is...

LONNIE REX

He is the president and founder of The David Livingstone Foundation for International Relief in Tulsa. He found his personal answer to this question one day when he was in Asia. He shared the story with me as we were visiting together.

"I was in Korea as the war was ending and was told about some hurting children at an orphanage located in a nearby barn. I went there, and the sight was pitiful. Ninety-five kids living on straw floors. They were hungry and living in the dark because all their bulbs had burned out. Mrs. Lee, a precious lady who was caring for the children, told me they

"Anyone could
help one
orphan."
— Lonnie Rex

had no money, were living on meals of rice, and that by the next day all the food for the children would be gone.

"I sent one of my associates back to town to get light bulbs and food for the children. I knew the food would only last a few weeks. I asked myself, 'What could I do to help these children?'

I didn't have the finances to support nearly one hundred orphans. Then it suddenly dawned on me. Maybe I couldn't sponsor an entire orphanage, but anyone could help one orphan! All I had to do was find a sponsor for each orphan.

"Quickly, I started calling friends around the globe. It was exhausting, and at times embarrassing. Finally I had found a sponsor for each of the ninety-five children."

That was just the beginning. More than forty years later, Lonnie Rex is still helping orphans. Only now, it's thousands of them around the world. He impacted this generation and found his personal destiny, because he was willing to demonstrate Jesus' love by releasing what was in his hands.

I HAVE NO HANDS BUT YOUR HANDS

During World War II, a beautiful statue of Jesus was badly damaged by the bombing in France.

After the war ended, the villagers gathered up the pieces of the broken statue, which had been located in front of their church, and began to repair it.

Every part of the statue was repaired but one — the hands were never found. Some of the people said, "What good is our Jesus without hands?"

That statement gave one of them an idea. At his suggestion, they made a plaque and attached it to the statue with these words: "I have no hands but your hands!"

One day a visitor saw the handless statue and wrote a poem:

> I have no hands but your hands,
> to do my work today.
> I have no feet but your feet,
> to lead souls on the way.
> I have no tongue but your tongue,
> to tell them how I died.
> I have no help but your help,
> to bring them to God's side.

When Jesus walked on the earth He was constantly using His hands to bring healing, help, and compassion to hurting people. He commanded us to do the same: "...the works that I do shall [ye] do also..." (John 14:12).

The way we accomplish this task does not necessarily require any massive ceremony or program. Jesus outlined it quite clearly when He said that when we have done anything unto one of the least of our brothers or sisters, we have done it unto Him.

MAKE YOUR OWN HEADLINE

What are your hands doing to help others?

_____

"...Inasmuch as ye have done it unto one of the least of these...ye have done it unto me."
Matthew 25:40

_____

Wife Victimized By Chiseling Romeo

It was a whirlwind romance. They met in the summer and several weeks later flew to Reno to be married.

Now he has left and she has discovered that he had stolen $50,000 through forged documents and unauthorized credit card purchases.

Police said the wife never saw any of her husband's identification cards or licenses and now believes his name was an alias. She doesn't know much about him, other than his physical description and that he played the piano and drank coke.

As foolish as it may seem for this lady to have married someone she hardly knew, it is not uncommon for a variation of this scenario to transpire in the marketplace. It occurs when two virtual strangers come together financially.

As with the lady in the article, the results oftentimes are disastrous. So warns...

JIM GUINN

Jim Guinn of Dallas, Texas, is a CPA, noted author, and speaker. The following are some of his warning signs of dangerous investments.

Don't Be The Next Victim

1. SOUNDS TOO GOOD: If the investment sounds unbelievable or unreal, then it probably is.

2. REQUIRES ADVANCE CASH: Be wary if the person promoting the investment requires cash before furnishing you all the details of the investment.

3. MUST BE KEPT TOP SECRET: If the promoter discourages you from talking to your financial advisor, CPA, or attorney because of the secretive nature of the investment, be cautious.

4. PRODUCES NO TRACK RECORD: Always insist on receiving verifiable references from associates and/or previous investors. If these are not available, then don't invest.

5. IT'S NOW OR NEVER: When the promoter tries to rush you to invest because the investment opportunity is limited and "going fast," be very careful.[1]

Power Point

"Safe investments seldom offer exorbitant rates of return."
— Jim Guinn

MAKE YOUR OWN HEADLINE

What policies do you currently have in place to prevent yourself from making bad investments?

Be ye not unequally yoked together with unbelievers....
2 Corinthians 6:14

Gold Found In Hotel Mini-Bars

Hotels across the country are finding that mini-bars can deliver maxi-profits. It's like finding gold in the refrigerator.

Most people think that a hotel mini-bar is supposed to be like their refrigerator at home. At night it is easy to grab a Coke, a bag of chips, or some other quick snack.

Now many hotels throughout the country are taking the concept of mini-bars one step further. Souvenirs such as golf balls, sunglasses, T-shirts, disposable cameras, and inflated beach balls, as well as drugstore items such as lip balm, bug spray, antacids, and suntan lotion, are sharing cramped mini-bar space with the soft drinks and nuts.

These added products are producing extra profits for hotels.

As an example, Hilton Hotels Corporation has found that guests who use its mini-bar units spend an average of $3.40/night. The hotel chain averages more than $14 million in annual sales from its mini-bars and makes a profit of around 38 percent or approximately 5.32 million dollars.[1]

These hotels are using a powerful income-enhancing strategy that I refer to as "product-added increase."

PRODUCT-ADDED INCREASE

"Product-added increase" is based on the concept that by "piggybacking" new products or offerings with existing products or offerings, additional sales and profits can be created.

For instance, years ago when I opened my Chrysler dealership in Southern California, I soon came to realize that we needed to create additional sources of income to our normal profits from car sales and service.

I did some checking around and found that there were some optional services we could make available to our customers at the time of sale that would produce extra income for us. Soon we were offering extended warranties, life and accident insurance policies, and vehicle service contracts. The income from these extra offerings became so significant that there were some months that the extra profits made from them was the difference between the dealership being in the black or the red.

I have noticed this "product-added" concept being used by most airline reservation agents. When booking a plane reservation for a customer by phone, the agent asks if he can also assist with car rental reservations. That simple question produces millions of dollars in extra income for the airlines every year.

Another example of a company which makes use of this profitable strategy is Avon. In 1971, the well-known cosmetics firm added jewelry to its product lineup. In less than two years, it had become the largest distributor of fashion jewelry in the world.[2]

By adding some extra products, my friend Peter Lowe — who is billed as "America's Premiere Success Seminar Conductor" — used this concept and greatly increased his profits per seminar by adding VIP seating and celebrity lunches.

You may be able to greatly increase your profits by adding extra products and/or services to your line up.

MAKE YOUR OWN HEADLINE

Are there products or services that you could "piggyback" with your existing products to increase your "bottom-line" profitability?

"...I am the Lord thy God which teacheth thee to profit...."
Isaiah 48:17

Vultures Attack During Graduation Ceremony

Students and guests fled for their lives as a swarm of fifty or more vultures swooped down and attacked the crowd.

This attack was very abnormal because vultures seldom attack in situations where there are large numbers. They also avoid attacking strength but usually prey on weakness.

PAT BOONE

He felt like he was being attacked by vultures as a result of a financial crisis in which he found himself.

He and a friend had purchased the franchise rights to operate a professional basketball team in the newly formed American Basketball Association.

The team was losing money and, as he put it, "eating him alive" financially. However, he wasn't paying much attention to it until he received a frantic call from his accountant about the team. There had been an incredible overdraft, and the bank was demanding that he come up with $700,000 within 24 hours!

When Pat called home to inform his wife Shirley about the problem, she told him that her dad, country-western singer Red Foley, had just died.

"You fellas don't understand. The bank is in the hands of God."

Pat scraped up the $700,000. However, the team continued to lose money by the trainload.

His nerves began to bother him, causing the skin to literally peel off his fingers. His doctor told him, "I can give you something to put on it, but it's coming from the inside."

Faced with immense monetary problems, Pat brought in top-flight lawyers and financial experts who worked night and day to discover a solution. Although his advisors could help, he soon realized that only God could solve the problem.

The pressure of the situation caused him to experience a spiritual renewal.

"I found myself searching for a closeness to God," he remembers. "As I prayed, I began to sense the Lord's presence in a remarkable way. I released the worry of the situation to Him. It was an uplifting, joyous time.

"However, it was hard for me to smile the day the bank sent me a letter demanding me to immediately send a check for another $1,300,000! To think that I could find $1,300,000 immediately was laughable.

"The next day my attorneys called and said that the team had to file for bankruptcy, and I probably would too.

"'Fellas, thanks. You've done your best,' I said. 'Now that we give up, watch! God is going to solve this problem.'

"My attorneys said, 'You don't understand. It's out of our hands. It's now in the hands of the bank.'

"I boldly replied, 'You fellas don't understand. The bank is in the hands of God.'"[1]

Pat continued to pray and believe God for a miracle.

Noted pastor Charles Stanley says that faith is the Holy Spirit's signal to go into action.

That was certainly true in Pat's case. Two days later a man from Washington, DC, whom he had never met, bought the team for almost two million dollars.

Have you developed the willingness or ability to work hard, but release the pressure to God? Are you in a situation which you need to let go to God?

"David said, The Lord will deliver me out of the hand
of mine enemy."
1 Samuel 17:37 (author's paraphrase)

Resident Fighting Bugs Loses Apartment

A woman who was enraged by cockroaches in her apartment sparked an explosion when she fumigated it with nine pesticide foggers. The fire department officials at the scene said, "That was probably eight too many."

The apartment no longer has any bugs. It also no longer has windows, and a large crack now divides the living room ceiling.

Do you have a bug problem? Some people do and don't even know it. I'm not referring to dealing with insects, but with being "informationally bugged." By that I mean others tapping into your data, correspondence, and/or communications without your knowledge to take personal and/or business information.

CONSIDER THIS...

"They had us all bugged," stated the police chief about the Colombian drug cartel. He reported that the spying network was so sophisticated that it used devices even the intelligence agencies didn't have. The cartel succeeded in bugging the phones of the police department and top government officials including the defense, interior, and justice ministers.

It could even intercept calls on half the telephones in Bogota, a city of seven million people.

You might think that a problem of "bugs" only concerns drug dealers and police in South America. How about this report?

BUGS ON PLANES

Recently, one foreign country's security intelligence agency warned its top business people not to fly a certain European air carrier. The reason: they discovered that the airline's first and business class sections were bugged — electronically bugged. Not only that, but undercover agents were posing as flight attendants in order to steal corporate secrets from unsuspecting business travelers.[1]

These espionage stories of "bugs" still might not seem relevant to you — but how about this one?

This year a class-action law suit was filed on behalf of 1,500 black employees of an oil company. The suit alleges that certain executives vilified black employees during staff meetings. One of those in attendance at the meetings neglected to tell his colleagues that he had a tiny tape recorder hidden in his jacket.

Or even closer to home. The last time you signed on the Internet, someone could have watched what you did, noticed what you said, or recorded what you bought, and then shared that information with various marketers or other interested parties.

The point of all these stories is to cause you to realize that the more successful you become, the more vulnerable you are to "bugging." Therefore, greater importance must be given to protecting the confidentiality of conversations and documents.

If you are like many achievers, this information and more may be available to competitors, to dishonest or super-ambitious employees, or to anyone else who might visit your office after hours, steal your briefcase, or snatch your laptop computer.

If your company relies on proprietary information to maintain a competitive edge in the marketplace, I would strongly suggest that you conduct a "security vulnerability inspection." Develop systems and policies that will minimize your risk of unintended information distribution.

Remember, Jesus Himself was betrayed by Judas who was one of His inner circle.

This is important. A "bug problem" could cost you a lot more than a damaged apartment; it could cost you your business.

MAKE YOUR OWN HEADLINE

What safeguards do you have in place to protect valuable information and data from unauthorized distribution? Do you or your company have a security awareness program?

Discretion will protect you, and understanding will guard you.
Proverbs 2:11 NIV

Fresh ideas, new energy, and increased living lie ahead for those individuals willing to create a thinking flood.

Charles Stanley says, "Over the years we have all been programmed to think a certain way."

Stephen Covey believes that for most people this thinking, in the economic arena, is founded on what he calls a "scarcity mentality." He says, "These people see life as having only so much, as though there were only one pie out there. And if someone were to get a bigger piece of the pie, it would mean less for everybody else."

Covey continues, "People with a scarcity mentality...have a hard time being genuinely happy for the success of other people....It's almost as if something is being taken from them if someone else receives special recognition, gain, or has remarkable success or achievement."[1]

That is why Super-Achiever Seminar conductor Bernie Dohrman declares, "For a person to change their life, they must first change their thinking."

But how does one do that?

Desire alone won't do it. Attending seminars, listening to tapes, and reading books won't do it either. However, if a person simultaneously floods himself with these things, all of them working together can make the difference.

Let me share with you how my life changed when I learned the powerful secret of...

HOW TO CREATE A FLOOD

As a young man I had achieved a good level of economic success but was constantly battling with negative expectations, unclear priorities, emotional instability, and fear of failure.

I was determined once and for all to drive "lack thinking" out of my life. I got my Bible out and started studying the stories in which financial miracles and breakthroughs occurred. I also searched to discover key verses on personal and economic success and overcoming lack. I wrote these verses on three-by-five cards and carried them. Every free moment I had, I pulled them out of my pocket and confessed them again and again to drive them into my core belief system.

Then, I purchased twelve tape recorders and placed them throughout our home — in all of our bedrooms and bathrooms, the kitchen, the laundry room — and in both cars. Every available waking moment I devoured motivational tapes and cassettes on Biblical economics.

I also realized that I needed to change some of my close associations. I could no longer afford to regularly associate with ungodly acquaintances or poverty thinking friends, with their negative attitudes and their unwillingness to change. I was determined to rise to a higher level of thinking and living. No one was going to hold me down.

Soon, I began to notice a change on the inside of me. Creativity, power, faith, positive affirmations, and fresh new dreams began to spring from my inner being.

A short time later, I had to fight my way through a season of unbelievable financial pressure in my business. I was able to survive only because prior to those attacks, I had taken the time and effort to flood my mind with faith and life-changing Biblical truths.

In addition, my marriage and family relationships took on a new stability, improved communication, and fresh love.

Also, a hunger and appreciation developed in the spiritual area of my life. In many ways, I became a different and much improved person.

From that time to this, I have led an overcoming and victorious life. I have experienced innumerable situations of financial increase and supernatural favor, have successfully raised five children. and have impacted countless numbers of lives through my speaking. In addition, I have been able to raise and/or contribute hundreds of thousands of dollars for the poor and needy, as well as to continually bless my church.

You too can experience greater stability and significance, if you will take the time and effort to create a positive-based, lack-defeating, increase-thinking flood.

MAKE YOUR OWN HEADLINE

How active and creative are you in unleashing the restorative powers of the Bible in your life? How would an absence of scarcity thinking affect your life?

...as he [a person] thinketh in his heart, so is he....
Proverbs 23:7

Woman Stung By Thousands Of Mad Bees

A woman who was attempting to close the door at an abandoned house was attacked by a cloud of angry bees and had to be rushed to the hospital.

A re you fed up with too many "B's" — average outcomes of events in your life?

Experts say one of the best ways to improve the odds for a positive outcome is through increased preparation.

A good example of how superior preparation opened the door of opportunity is found in the life of...

MARY LOU RETTON

Backstage, Mary Lou is just as exciting and vibrant as she was in the 1984 Olympics when she won five Olympic medals. Who could ever forget her perfect score of 10 in the final event, making her the first American ever to win an individual gold medal in Olympic gymnastics?

Proper preparation is one of her secrets to success. She says, "I knew that I had to be the best in the gym or I would not be the best in competition."

"One of my teammates was injured before an international meet," she continues. "The coach turned to me and said, 'You're in.' I was ready for that moment and was on the team from that day on."

Look at what other super-achievers say about the importance of proper preparation:

ARE YOU READY?

"Talent alone will not make you a success. Neither will being at the right place at the right time, unless you are ready. The important question is, 'Are you ready?'"

— Johnny Carson

"The game may be played in a stadium, but it is won or lost on the practice field."[1]

— Former NFL coach Joe Gibbs

"Success occurs when opportunity meets preparation."

— Zig Ziglar

"Whatever you are ready for normally shows up."

— George Burns

"Anything you choose to do in life, you'll only be as good as you are in the practice drill."[2]

— Tom Hopkins

"You must battle at a high level in order to compete at a high level."[3]

— NFL Head Coach Norv Turner
Washington Redskins

"The will to succeed is important, but what is more important is the will to prepare."[4]

— Head Basketball Coach Bobby Knight
Indiana University

"Before everything else, getting ready is the secret of success."[5]

— Henry Ford

"Good fortune is what happens when opportunity meets with preparation."[6]

— Thomas Edison

How prepared are you for the position and/or dream that you desire? In what ways could better preparation increase your opportunities?

"...thou hast been faithful over a few things, I will make thee
ruler over many things...."
Matthew 25:21

School Says Occupants Stink

The "Stink Posse" at the local elementary school is giving up. For over a month, staff members have been grappling with a smelly problem in one of their buildings.

Apparently skunks have been living around, and releasing odors in, an area near a drainage system next to one of the classroom complexes. Heating intake vents have been carrying the odorless smell to all parts of the building. When teachers and students began complaining of headaches and difficulty concentrating, skunk traps were set, but were ineffective. School officials are now "Calling Foul" and conceding defeat. They have decided to hire professionals to combat the "Skunk Invasion."

The above problem can occur not only with skunks, but also with negative friends and critical associates. When these "stinky varmints" start hanging around, they can also cause headaches and loss of concentration.

The problem is caused by the fact that over time, the thinking, attitudes, spirits, and even scents of those nearest you can become attached to you and your life.

If problem friends are stinking up your life, you have three options: 1) Choose to continue the relationship, 2) try to change the conditions it produces, or 3) separate yourself from the annoyance.

Here are some comments from my friends on this subject:

ABOUT FRIENDS

"Your accomplishments do not make you great, it's your friends."

— General Norman Schwarzkopf
Retired U.S. General

"Find friends who have strengths you do not possess."

— Mark Victor Hansen
Best-selling Author

> "My choice to change my closest friends was a turning point in my life."
> — John Mason

"One of the reasons we've survived our critics is that our friends helped keep us going."[1]

— George Bush

"Show me a person's friends and I'll show you their character."[2]

— Ed Cole
Men's Movement Leader

"My choice to change my closest friends was a turning point in my life."[3]

— John Mason
Best-selling Author

"The things that you most admire about your friends are probably their attitudes."[4]

— John C. Maxwell

"To be a winner you must associate with winners."[5]

— Dexter Yager
Amway Crown Distributor

MAKE YOUR OWN HEADLINE

Take inventory of your closest friends. What things do you admire most about them? Which of these qualities do you possess?

He who walks with wise men will be wise, but the companion of fools
will suffer harm.
Proverbs 13:20 NASB

Fire Guts Restaurant

A raging fire completely destroyed The Dwarf House Restaurant last evening.

S. TRUETT CATHY

The president and founder of the popular Chick-Fil-A restaurant chain faced one of his greatest crises. It was back in 1946. His second restaurant, The Dwarf House, was burning down. It seemed that his dreams were literally going up in smoke. To make matters worse, that same week doctors found cancerous polyps in his colon.

Today Truett says, "No matter what lay in the future, I knew that I could face it."[1] He could do so because he had a confidence in himself and his Lord. He firmly believes, "Fifty percent of the battle ends when you make up your mind."[2]

He quickly overcame the health problems and was soon rebuilding the restaurant, only this time it would be different. He decided to open it as the area's first self-service fast food restaurant specializing in chicken.

Sales were mediocre until he discovered that by removing the bone and skin from the chicken breast he could cut the cooking time in half. This could greatly decrease his expenses. He then came up with the idea of

"Fifty percent
of the battle
ends when you
make up your
mind."
— S. Truett Cathy

putting this breast on a bun and adding special seasoning. The Chick-Fil-A sandwich was born.

Today there are more than 600 Chick-Fil-A outlets across America, bringing in the industry's top sales income per unit, even though every store is closed on Sundays.

I visited with Truett on a recent trip to Washington, DC. He is a generous giver to charities and churches. He says that if one will walk hand in hand with God...

IT'S EASIER TO SUCCEED THAN TO FAIL

- "It's easier to succeed because success eliminates the agony and frustration of defeat."

- "It's easier to succeed because failure exacts a high price in terms of time when you have to do a job over."

- "It's easier to succeed because money spent to fail must be spent again to succeed."

- "It's easier to succeed because a person's credibility decreases with each failure, making it harder to succeed the second time around."

- "And it's easier to succeed because joy and excitement come from succeeding, whereas feelings of discouragement and discontent accompany failure."[3]

Truett truly believes, "If one will walk hand in hand with God, it is easier to succeed than to fail."[4]

MAKE YOUR OWN HEADLINE

Is there some change in methods or technique that could bring you increase?

_____

"...my yoke is easy, and my burden is light."
Matthew 11:30

_____

Exploding Can Theory Wins

A local engineering student won the regional competition in mechanical engineering with his explanation of why a soda can exploded while sitting on a shelf.

It was Abraham Lincoln who said that a person's determination to succeed is more important than any other thing.

You are on the road to greater increase if, when faced with adversity or seemingly unsolvable obstacles, out of your inner being explode the words "I can."

Richard DeVos, co-founder of Amway Corporation, says, "The only thing that stands between a man and what he wants from life is often merely the will to try and the faith to believe that it is possible."

My friend, motivational speaker Les Brown, concurs: "You must know within yourself that if others can live their dreams, you can live yours too."[1]

"WE ARE ABLE"

The Bible tells the story of the tribe of Israel escaping from the bondage of Egypt and arriving on the banks of the Jordan River. Their leader, Moses, sent twelve spies to report on conditions in the Promised Land.

Ten returned with a negative report about giants and walled cities. Two, Joshua and Caleb, saw the challenges but instead focused on the God of miracles. The ten spies perished in the wilderness. They got what they believed. Joshua and Caleb possessed the land. They too got what they believed.

The only difference between Joshua and Caleb and the other ten spies was this "can-do attitude." The ten focused on the walled cities, the giants, and the fact that they were outnumbered. Joshua and Caleb saw those same things but declared that they didn't matter because the God Who had brought them out of the bondage of Egypt and parted the Red Sea was with them. They boldly stated, "We are able." (See Numbers 13.)

Many times in life it is not the problems you face that matters, it is your attitude towards them. It is important to remember that...

INCREASE COMES IN CANS

If you think you are beaten, you are;
If you think you dare not, you don't.
If you like to win, but you think you can't,
It is almost certain you won't.

If you think you'll lose, you've lost,
For out of the world you'll find
Increase begins with a fellow's believing —
It's all in his state of mind.

If you think you are outclassed, you are;
You've got to think higher to rise.
You've got to believe in yourself before
You can ever win the prize.

Life's battles don't always go
To the stronger or faster man;

But sooner or later, the man who wins
Is the man WHO THINKS HE CAN!

— Unknown

How could you put more exploding "cans of increase" into your life?

"...we are well able...."
Numbers 13:30

Getting A Head Start

Delicate time balance is required for planting lettuce. If the soil is too cold the seed won't germinate. If it is too warm the plant sends up a tall stalk which turns to weed. Lettuce doesn't thrive in summer but can do well again in the cool of fall.

RETIRED GENERAL NORMAN SCHWARZKOPF

The commander of Desert Storm joined Cindy, me, and my friend Peter Lowe for dinner following a recent success seminar in St. Louis.

Cindy asked him if he missed being in the military. He replied he did miss the camaraderie with the troops and the rich relationships he had in the military but that he was enjoying his new life.

Then he stated, "One of the secrets of my success is that I have learned that most positions in life are temporary and that life is a collection of seasons."

LEARN TO RECOGNIZE THE SEASONS

This powerful concept, which is well understood by farmers, is often not fully realized by achievers. Each of us must train ourselves to think of life in terms of seasons which require different actions, obligations, and responses.

The changing of seasons determines when a sower plants. It also dictates what clothes a mother buys for her children, whether a stockbroker buys or sells, and whether a vacationer heads for the mountain slopes for skiing or the mountain lake for sunning.

Seasons are a part of life. In nature, winter is the season of survival, while spring is the season of increase.

CELEBRATE THE SEASONS OF YOUR LIFE

As an example, Cindy and I are currently going through a time when two of our children (Wendy and Crystol) still live at home while attending the university and working for us. We tremendously enjoy our time with them. However, based upon the number of sharp young men who continue to phone and call at our residence, we know it won't be long until our time with the single girls at home will end.

Many parents get depressed and bored or feel lonely and unfulfilled when their children leave home. Psychologists refer to this phenomenon as "the empty nest syndrome." It takes place when parents fail to see it as the end of one type of relationship (season) but the beginning of another (counselors, friends, parents-in-law, grandparents) and enriched time together.

Learn to recognize the changing seasons. Better yet, learn to anticipate them and celebrate them. As you begin to flow with the seasons of life, it will reduce stress, release fresh increase, and give you a head start.

MAKE YOUR OWN HEADLINE

What can you do to bring "seasonal thinking" into your life?

To every thing there is a season....
Ecclesiastes 3:1

Bobbies Like Their Helmets

London police don't want to give up their traditional hard-shell helmets. They are refusing to consider wearing the traditional American-style soft caps. However, they are considering a new headgear that looks like a bicycle helmet and can withstand a blow from a baseball bat.

England is an island country that has been attacked many times. Therefore, it is understandable that not only do the London police think in terms of defensive armament, so does the leadership of the country. This became quite evident during a time that Cindy and I had lunch with Great Britain's former prime minister, Margaret Thatcher.

LADY THATCHER

Lady Thatcher, who is a very charming, bright and articulate woman, was Britain's first-ever female prime minister. During her three terms in office, that nation began to rebound economically as state-owned companies and government-furnished rental homes were replaced with private ownership. Also, Britain started to regain her tarnished reputation as a world power under Lady Thatcher's courageous leadership.

Her defensive mindset came to light when she stated, "Evil and conflict will always be with us, so we must keep our defenses strong. It is only with strong defenses that freedom can be maintained. For every offensive weapon that your enemy possesses, you must have a defensive counterpart or you will eventually be defeated."

Here are some of Lady Thatcher's other...

INSIGHTFUL COMMENTS

- GOVERNMENT: "When a government allows its people and enterprises to flourish, then the country will flourish."

- STRENGTH: "A bully has no respect for a weakling, and the only way to stop a bully is not to be weak."

- FREEDOM: "You can not have freedom without laws, rules, and responsibilities."

- HOME: "It should be a base of operations, but it must also be a refuge."

- OPPOSITION: "In battle sometimes you must be more concerned about the knives at your back than the guns in front of you."

- BATTLES: "You may have to fight a battle more than once to win it."

- ECONOMICS: "The way to recovery is through profits."

- PERSONAL ATTACKS: "People can be vicious. Don't pay too much attention to them or you will get a complex about yourself."

- SPIRITUALITY: "It is only in recognizing that people are spirit beings that individuals achieve importance and significance."

MAKE YOUR OWN HEADLINE

In what ways would increasing your "defensive protection mindset" change your decisions and/or lifestyle — economically, maritally, physically, spiritually?

Neither give place to the devil.
Ephesians 4:27

Arab Sheik Buys 40 College Degrees

A rich oil baron who cannot read or write has received more than 40 degrees, six of them doctorates, from a university he built in his hometown.

The receiving of college diplomas, medals, awards, or citations is very important to many people. Not only do such honors furnish an element of personal pride and recognition, but oftentimes they cause a future increase in income in the marketplace.

Because of the power and prestige that is attached to winning or being honored with awards, people will often put forth extraordinary effort to receive them — sometimes even resorting to devious means to do so.

Not long ago a Congressman was accused of falsely stating that he graduated from college as a member of the honor society Phi Beta Kappa in order to increase his prestige. The disclosure prevented him from running for re-election.

The U.S. Navy's top admiral recently committed suicide after it was allegedly reported that he had worn battle citations on his uniform that he had not rightfully earned.

What should an individual do if she believes that she and her team members are legitimately deserving of recognition for personal achievement for which no such award exists? If she thinks like my daughter, Wendy, she creates an award.

WENDY JOY HARRISON

She has always been a strong-willed, determined, bright, and innovative daughter. She graduated from the university with great grades. There is no doubt in my mind that had it not been for her innumerable absences caused by travels with her parents for seminars and holidays, she could have graduated with highest honors.

Although Wendy's schedule did not allow her to consistently pursue the highest academic achievement, she did have time to maximize her gifts and talents on her senior paper project, which was more short term in nature. She led a team which did a masterful job of analyzing a local business and coming up with creative ways to increase its sales and profits.

The paper was so good that it was declared the best senior paper by the school of business and was submitted for state competition.

Wendy was ecstatic about this honor which showcased superior marketing and management skills — until she discovered that no formal recognition or award was given by the school for this accomplishment. Since the school of business gave recognition to other academic accomplishments, and since this project was such a major undertaking, she could not understand why it was not treated similarly.

Instead of accepting this "non-recognition status quo," she began the process of trying to get the recognition she believed the task merited. She talked to her teachers and went through the various academic channels until an idea was born. She prepared a proposal for the school to offer a Best Senior Paper Award to be presented each year as part of the award presentations at the school of business hooding ceremonies.

Soon her proposal reached the head of the business school, along with a sample award which she had prepared on her computer. The dean responded, "It's never been done before...but why not?"

A few weeks later, on graduation weekend, our family attended the hooding ceremony. Several students received academic and merit awards. Many parents radiated with pride at the accomplishments of their offspring. However, none could have been any prouder than we were, because our daughter not only received an award but had the innovativeness and determination to create an award — for her team, herself, and all those who would come after her.

MAKE YOUR OWN HEADLINE

How much more could you accomplish if you were bolder in carrying out your ideas? What has it cost you not to pursue harder what you know to be worthwhile goals and dreams?

...do good; seek peace, and pursue it.
Psalm 34:14

ROGER STAUBACH

The former Dallas Cowboys legend retired as one of the NFL's all-time great quarterbacks, having led his team to four Superbowls over an eight-year span, while becoming one of the top-ranked passers of all time.

His move toward retirement came after a Pittsburgh lineman hit him so hard he spun around and found himself "flat" on the earth. That was his sixth concussion for the season — and his last one ever.

We spoke together at a seminar in Oklahoma City. I was impressed not only with his intelligence, wit, and charm, but also with his clean-cut image.

As far as his football honors, wealth, and fame are concerned, Roger believes that everything we do on earth is temporary. He says, "The only permanent thing is a relationship with Christ. That is the bond which extends beyond this earth."

Roger is proud to be known as a Christian but he is bothered by the dull and one-dimensional image that is often put forth by others of the Christian lifestyle.

Here are his views on...

THE CHRISTIAN STEREOTYPE

"Many people act as if the things I believe in, and the life I live, reduce the enjoyment of living when compared to the playboy, 'whatever makes you feel good, do it' philosophy. To me that's incredible. Those whose lifestyle is a constant parade of jumping from this to that, who always think the grass is greener somewhere else, only find insecurity. Insecurity leads them to misery and oftentimes the using of chemical means to take care of their lives.

"Sure, it might provide a temporary euphoria to have one-night stands with any woman you run into or by taking drugs. But none of those experiences have permanent value or merit. They are the here-today, gone-tomorrow sensations, whereas God is today, tomorrow, and forever.

"I don't feel I'm missing any of life's pleasures or joys. I'm a happy man. I'm happy with who I am, with what I am, with my wife, my family, and my God.

"Peace of mind and good relationships with those at home — and with our Creator — form the foundation of a happy existence. From there one can really enjoy life."

MAKE YOUR OWN HEADLINE

What are you doing to increase your relationships at home? With your Creator? What kind of image and testimony do you put forth?

For I am not ashamed of the gospel of Christ; for it is the power of God....
Romans 1:16

Traffic Jam On The Road To Success

A local success seminar packed the city arena and caused a gridlock on area streets and freeways.

H is very presence in a city fills the largest convention centers and creates epic traffic jams. He is an inspirational speaker. He is hot. He is the best. He is...

PETER LOWE

In just ten years from start-up to number one in America, my buddy Peter Lowe has become a "success sensation." His life and seminars — attracting audiences of 20,000 and more — have been featured in *Time*, *Selling*, *New Man*, and *People* magazines and reported on CNN.

It was shortly after hearing me speak at a meeting in Vancouver, Canada, in 1981, that Peter made the decision to become a sales trainer. He determined that his life would make an impact — a difference — in the lives of others.

In the early years, Peter had to memorize his presentations word for word but he was diligent, faithful, and committed. Even in the face of

"The problem with most achievers is that they don't feed themselves enough."

unbelievable obstacles and intense competition, each year he got better, and bigger, and bigger.

From my notes on some of our times together here is...

PETER LOWE ON SUCCESS

1. PERSEVERE: "A person cannot become really successful in anything until he determines that he will not quit. Winners don't give up — they get up."

2. BE DILIGENT: "Do what needs to be done. Watch the details. I personally analyze at least 30 pages of computer reports every day in order to maximize the attendance and income of each seminar."

3. THINK PIGGYBACK: "We increased our revenues by hundreds of thousands of dollars per year by adding special celebrity speakers, a VIP seating section, idea-exchange lunches, and program options to each seminar's program."

4. SUSTAIN PROPER INPUT: "The problem with most achievers is that they do not feed themselves enough — mentally and spiritually. Keep yourself on a consistent and regular feeding program of books, tapes, seminars, and fellowship with other achievers."

5. BE AWARE OF TIMING: "There is a right time to change, to introduce new speakers and/or programs for optimum results. The timing of when something is done is oftentimes as important as what is done."

6. BE CONSISTENT: "Don't keep reinventing yourself. Discover what you are to do and then stick with it. You may change your tactics and methods, but stay with your core principles and calling."

7. PLAN LONG TERM: "Success takes time. There must be seasons of sowing before there will be seasons of reaping. I am much more interested in where I will be in five years than I am in the next seminar."

What is the long view of your business? Your life? Is what you are sowing today going to give you the harvest that you desire later? What are you doing to sustain proper motivational input?

Wise men lay up knowledge....
Proverbs 10:14

The Outback Restaurant chain opened a new steak house across from the mall.

Reading the above headline about the "outback" caused me to remember an amazing marketing strategy used by many successful individuals and corporations.

In the sales arena, follow-up or repeat sales to the same customer are often referred to as "outback" or "back-end" sales. Normally these sales can cause a much greater profit to be realized by a seller, because the initial expenses of getting the customer have already been met. Also, hopefully a positive business relationship has already been created.

Look at what these corporations discovered about "back-end" sales:

- Ford Motor Company estimates that it costs five times (500 percent) as much to attract a new customer as it does to retain a current one.

- Home Depot found that its average customer spends an average of $38 per sale. However, based upon a lifetime of doing business with the same customer, that amount could soar to $25,000 per customer.

- Continental Airlines found that the long-term value of a customer standing before an agent could be as much as 100 times the amount of that day's ticket transaction.

THE SECRET TO INCREASED SALES

My friend Ken Kerr — one of America's top image consultants and the creative project manager for the construction of Walt Disney's Epcot Center in Florida — says that "repeat customers are the best source of customer increase." He shared a story on the value of repeat sales at a seminar we held together in California:

"One of my clients offered to sell a collection of coins to new customers for 19 dollars. He actually lost a few dollars on every sale. Over 50,000 people responded.

"The next month nearly 10,000 of those same people bought an 'after-sale' collection at $1,000 each. My client made $2,000,000 profit on the 'back-end after-sale.'

"In addition, three months later he resolicited the original 50,000 people who had bought the 19-dollar coin sets. About 250 of them bought $1,000 more of coins every quarter. That made him another $50,000 a year in 'back-end' profits.

"That's not all. Later he resolicited those 10,000 people who bought something for $1,000. About 1,500 of them bought more coins averaging $5,000 per order. This made him another $1,500,000.

"There's still more. Those 1,500 customers continued ordering, creating extra income every year. All of this from 'back-end sales' that began with a 19-dollar offer."

Tom Peters teaches sales people to consider every customer to be a potential lifelong relationship, generating word-of-mouth references as well as future business.

Ken also believes that the secret is this: "Do not look at customers as one-time sales. Go back to them for repeat business. In sales, it's what's 'outback' that matters most."

MAKE YOUR OWN HEADLINE

Do you have additional products and/or services you could offer your new and/or existing customers? How could this positively affect your cash flow?

—————————————

"...I will give thee...the hidden riches of secret places...."
Isaiah 45:3

—————————————

Violent Explosion Rips Heart Of Nation

A truck bomb exploded at a federal building killing scores of people and destroying the sense of security of many Americans.

The bomb that exploded in Oklahoma City in April 1995 not only blew up a building, it also shattered part of the belief system of most Americans. In an instant, the perceived innocence and safety of this country was shaken at its roots. This tragedy was not happening in Northern Ireland, the Middle East, or Japan. It was taking place in Mid-America.

The average person cannot begin to fathom the sense of despair experienced by those who lost a loved one in the blast. All we know is that God promises that during these difficult times He will undergird and sustain those who turn to Him for guidance and support. In Joshua 1:5 NIV He says, "...I will never leave you nor forsake you."

Each of us, at some time, is going to experience times of personal loss and unexpected tragedy. It might be an accident to a friend or relative, the death of a loved one, a national catastrophe such as this bombing, or the assassination of a great leader such as John F. Kennedy or Martin Luther King, Jr.

If you find yourself going through a difficult time, remember that help can be found in the Bible (particularly in the Psalms) and through being empowered by the Holy Spirit (through prayer and praise).

By "hooking onto" these supernatural sources of power, your inner strength can be reinforced.

Here is some additional advice from some who spoke at the...

BOMBING VICTIMS MEMORIAL SERVICE

Why do bad things happen to innocent people?

"The human heart is capable of almost limitless evil when cut off from God and moral law."

— Rev. Billy Graham

How do we help with others' grief?

"Tell family members that we love them, we care, and we're very sorry."

— Dr. Rod Masteller

How do we heal the hurting we all experience?

"A tree takes a long time to grow, and wounds take a long time to heal, but we must begin."

— President Bill Clinton

How do we rebuild our own lives?

"Experience is not what happens to us. It is what we choose to do with what happens to us."

— Rev. Carlton Pearson

The underlying message from each of these leaders is for us to take the negative experience, memorialize it, learn from it, but then move on with life.

Use such occasions as a time to reexamine your priorities, evaluate what you are doing to help others, and then empower yourself to live to the fullest.

MAKE YOUR OWN HEADLINE

Since in every life there is a time to grieve and a time to heal, are there hurts from your past that need to change from grieving time to healing time? Is there someone who needs your love and compassion?

And the peace of God, which transcends all understanding, will guard your hearts and your minds in Christ Jesus.
Philippians 4:7 NIV

Blackout Blinds Jets

A power failure knocked out radar screens and radios at a major air traffic control center leaving airborne jets with no one to guide them.

A member of the New York Jets football team experienced a "black-out" of a different nature during a football game.

DENNIS BYRD

Dennis remembers lying there flat on his back on the turf and looking up. As the tingling in his body slowly subsided, his eyes gradually regained their focus on the gray New Jersey sky.

All he needed to do was push himself off the grass as he had done a thousand times before. When he tried to get up, he felt something give way. He heard it too, a grinding and crunching at the top of his spine. It was then he realized that he had broken his neck.

Author of the inspirational book, *Rise and Walk*,[1] Dennis shares the forces that enabled him to overcome this tragedy.

The first was determination.

"Never give up is a lesson I had learned on the football field. I had learned to push and push and push and, when you feel like collapsing, to push some more. I knew what effort and determination could accomplish. I used this determination every minute I was in the hospitals and rehab rooms."

Another force that helped him was the love of his family and wife.

"They were beside me encouraging me when it counted most."

However, the most important force that undergirded him and gave him the power to "bounce back" was an awareness of the presence of God.

"In my weakness I was able to completely lay my entire life at Christ's feet putting it all in His hands.

"I could easily have been destroyed by what happened to me. I could easily have just fallen apart, but I had this secret ingredient — the power of God — helping me.

"That's the miracle. It's knowing that the Lord is with us even when we break...He can help to make us whole. I have always believed that and always will."

Dennis' body began to improve at what the staff has told him was an amazing rate. His muscular strength and control got better every day. Soon he could walk without even a limp and was benching over 100 pounds — and lifting 250 pounds on the leg sled.

Although his football playing days are over, Dennis is living a vibrant and happy life sharing with people that they can overcome and win against most any adversity — if they never give up.

If you could hear God whispering to you, "I am with you," would you give up and quit?

———————————

...I will never leave you nor forsake you.
Joshua 1:5 NIV

———————————

As the first glow of early morning light began to brighten the dark skies, my wife and I glanced out of our bedroom windows toward the forest behind our home and the adjacent pool. We had just constructed the pool by carving out part of the hillside and building a large retaining wall. It is a breathtakingly beautiful site, as trees from the forest grace two of its sides.

However, that morning as I began to focus on the pool in the early dawn light, I noticed that something was floating and moving in it.

I raced downstairs and into the backyard. My eyes beheld an unbelievable sight. Apparently the torrential downpour had come at a time when frogs in the forest were beginning their new families. The fast-moving water had washed multitudes of frogs down from the hillside. There were scores and scores of them — big frogs and little frogs, live frogs and dead frogs, floating frogs and submerged frogs — all in my pool.

"WHAT ARE YOU GOING TO DO ABOUT THE FROGS?"

My wife followed me and saw the sight. She gasped and exclaimed, "What are you going to do about the frogs?"

"Get them out of here...now!" I replied.

In a short time I had rescued the live ones and disposed of the dead ones.

Having experienced that situation, I sympathize with other achievers who may have "frog problems" — although their frogs are of a different kind.

"Frogs" is the term I use to describe people who are so unstable that they seem unable to stay committed to anything. They are always "hopping around" from one job to another, one church to another, one set of friends to another. They seem to think that they can "find themselves" by jumping somewhere else. Worse yet, when they leap from one place to another, they normally "croak and croak" about what was wrong with the previous places and people they leaped from.

If you have friends and associates who are "frogs," it will negatively affect you. Their "croaking," constant hopping around, and lack of stability will impact your thinking, your attitude, and your effectiveness.

Don't get me wrong. Frogs are okay. They help make life interesting and are even fun to see and enjoy while going through the "jungle of life." However, they should reside in your garden or the forest. If you want to experience stability and maintain positiveness, there is no place for them in your "pool of influence."

Are there "frogs" in your life, hopping all around you and croaking about what's wrong with everything? Do you need to clean your "pool"? Why wait until tomorrow?

"...Intreat the Lord, that he may take away the frogs from me...."
Exodus 8:8

Train Stopped By Slimy Snails

A horde of snails, drawn out in overwhelming numbers by heavy rains, crawled onto the train rails, halting an express train when the train's wheels lost their grip because of the slime.

If you feel that a horde of multiple demands and overwhelming stress has caused you to experience procrastination and priority confusion and left you dead in your tracks, cheer up; there is hope.

DENIS WAITLEY

As Denis and I share the speaking stage together at conventions, I continue to marvel at his insight and knowledge in the areas of goal setting and time management. He says, "Many a person lives on Someday Isle, convinced that, 'Someday I'll do that' or 'Someday I'll go there.'

"The science of physics recognizes two kinds of inertia: Standing objects tend to remain stationary, and moving objects tend to stay in motion.

"Procrastination is stationary inertia. We aren't moving, so therefore we don't move! The first step toward success will be the biggest one...the beginning of movement."

SEVEN SECRETS TO OVERCOMING PROCRASTINATION

1. IDENTIFY: On a sheet of paper, write down the important activities you are delaying or have put on hold.

2. PICK ONE: Put the energy you have been directing toward excuses and not doing the task into one of the activities you have been avoiding.

3. PICK A TIME SLOT: Determine a specific time to begin or accomplish that one job or project.

4. COMMUNICATE: If what you are putting off involves other people, consult with them. Oftentimes what seems like a mountain is really only a mole hill when attacked.

5. ELIMINATE FEAR: Fear of the unknown can paralyze. Ask yourself, "What's the worst thing that could happen if I did this today?"

6. VISUALIZE: Vividly picture the joy and satisfaction you will feel once the task is finished.

7. JUST DO IT: What counts is quality of effort, not perfect results. Don't let yourself get bogged down. Each task or job completed will create momentum to continue.

I personally have found that the best way to break the habit of procrastination is to cultivate the reverse habit. A habit is nothing more than an action that has been repeated so many times that behavior is automatic. Therefore, by my action, I choose to create the opposite action, and soon it becomes the automatic response.

Today take some action to create the habit of motion.

What activities or projects have you been putting off? What simple, but specific steps can you take to begin?

...why stand ye gazing...?
Acts 1:11

To Suit Or Not To Suit?

The Miss America Pageant celebrated its 75th anniversary with an entertaining three-hour telecast.

However, a phone-in vote of TV viewers to determine whether to keep the traditional swimsuit competition that has been a part of the pageant since its inception upstaged much of what happened on stage. Nearly one million callers paid 50 cents each to phone in. Just short of 80 percent of them voted to keep the swimsuit tradition.

Over the years many people from various walks of life have asked me the question, "To suit or not to suit?" However, they were not referring to a swimsuit competition, but whether or not to file a lawsuit.

In our society, it is very easy to pursue a lawsuit if you believe you have been wronged. However, oftentimes the real question to ask is not can you, but should you?

TO SUE OR NOT TO SUE

Before pursuing a suit, consider the following:

1. OPPOSING PERSPECTIVE: Have you really attempted to see the issue from the other party's point of view and understand the opposing position or feelings?

2. ALTERNATIVE CAUSES OF ACTION: Has every other option been examined? Sometimes the only ones who get anything in a lawsuit are the attorneys.

3. CERTAINTY OF OUTCOME: Before investing your time and money in a suit, have you carefully weighed the strengths and legal options of the other side?

4. COLLECTIBILITY OF THE JUDGMENT: What good is it to win a judgment if the loser doesn't have any money or assets to attach or liquidate? How much extra time or effort will be involved in attempting to collect a judgment?

5. ATTENTION DEFICIT: How much is the pursuing of the suit going to cost you, your employees, and/or your company in lost money, time, focus, and energy? Could you generate more money by spending the same amount of time on "income increase" rather than on "suit recovery"?

6. SIDE EFFECTS: Will the pursuing of the suit cause you to be consumed for a season with negative issues that could trigger personal anger and hostility? If so, it could affect your health, marriage, relationships, and/or spiritual power.

7. FORGIVENESS: Would it not be better to convert this liability to "seed" for a future harvest and move on with life?

MAKE YOUR OWN HEADLINE

How many of the above points have you considered before pursuing a lawsuit? How might this consideration affect your decision?

There is a way that seems right...but in the end it leads to [destruction].
Proverbs 14:12 NIV

Ugly Lamp Brings Small Fortune

For 20 years a local man never gave much thought to a small lamp he had received as a gift. Now he's thinking about all the ways he can spend the money it fetched at an auction... $35,200!

The auctioneer called it "an ugly little lamp," but someone else placed a high value on it and purchased it for a seemingly unbelievable price. The buyer — who bid by phone from another state — said that he had a similar-looking Puff Point lamp and had been looking for a matching one for 20 years. He desired to obtain it so much that he was "willing to pay the price."

His comment brought afresh to my memory a story shared with me at a luncheon I recently enjoyed with a friend.

GARY RICHARDSON

He is called the "Top Gun of Oklahoma Attorneys" because he won the largest legal judgment in state history — $58 million. The story is about an incident that took place with Gary and his son several years ago.

ARE YOU WILLING TO PAY THE PRICE?

Gary's son Chuck was a first-year student at Baylor University in Waco, Texas, at the time. He called one day and asked permission to drop a math course before an upcoming big exam. He proceeded to tell Gary

"The issue is...are you willing to pay the price?"
— Gary Richardson

all the reasons why the course was too difficult and why he was not able to complete it.

Gary asked him to wait a couple of days before making the decision and suggested they meet in Dallas and discuss it over dinner the next night.

Gary drove to Dallas, and that night he told his son that he wasn't being honest with himself about what the issue really was. He stated, "Other students may only have to study a few hours to pass this math test next week. You may have to study 30, 50, or 70 hours to do well. But you are smart, and if you put in the study time, you can pass the exam. The issue isn't ability. It's simply, are you willing to study that much; are you willing to pay the price?"

Gary continued. "Another thing, son. All your life you'll be faced with similar hindrances. How you react to difficult challenges will develop a pattern that will either say, 'I will meet the challenge with God's help,' or 'I will cut and run.' This decision could be the beginning of your developing either one of these patterns. The decision is yours."

Gary's son decided to stay in the course, study, and take the test. He had to spend the entire weekend studying. The following Tuesday he took the test and made the top grade in the class.

Not only that, he has developed the habit pattern of facing adversity and being an overcomer. He is now a successful attorney practicing law with his dad in Tulsa.

MAKE YOUR OWN HEADING

What situation in your life are you currently facing that will help set a habit pattern of quitting or overcoming? When have you successfully overcome in the past? How did you do it?

"...we are well able to overcome...."
Numbers 13:30

Million Dollars Paid For Seat

A seat on the New York Stock Exchange recently sold for $1.15 million.

They are called "seats of power" and, as can be noted from the above article, they can be expensive. The term refers to seats where tremendous income can be produced, great influence can be given or received, and significant learning or enjoyment can take place.

For instance, it was reported that a dinner seat at the White House could be obtained for a $100,000 donation to the Democratic Party.

I have known people to pay up to $7,500 for a seat at a success seminar.

Recently, I was speaking in Atlanta while the World Series was being played there. Because of the city's enthusiasm, and the scarcity of tickets, game seats were selling for up to $1,000 each.

While it is true that "seats of power" normally become available as a direct result of the payment of money, sometimes they become available because of friends, favor, or divine intervention. Whatever their cause, achievers recognize these opportunities as special occasions that rate high in importance because of their potential influence or memories.

"Concentrate
on discovering
common points
of interest."
— Bob Harrison

Over the last several years, my wife and I have occupied dinner seats where we had the opportunity to meet, benefit from, and learn from some of the world's great leaders — from Margaret Thatcher to George Bush to Mikhail Gorbachev to Rev. Robert Schuller to NBC's Bob Costas.

Here are some things we have learned about these opportunities which can help to maximize their enjoyment and impact...

SEATS OF POWER

1. PREPARE IN ADVANCE: Study and obtain background information of key VIPs. Prepare questions to ask during conversations that will better enable you to increase learning and carry on intelligent conversations.

2. BE YOURSELF: More than anything else, celebrities love to associate with "real people" who are enjoyable to be around.

3. SHOW INTEREST: Maintain a caring attitude and act interested.

4. TALK MINIMALLY: Concentrate your conversation on friendly chat — asking for knowledge and/or discovering common points of interest.

5. BE TIME CONSCIOUS: Leaders are normally on tight schedules. They will relax and better enjoy their visit with you if they sense that you respect their time.

6. MAXIMIZE THE IMPACT: Get mementos — a program, picture, or autograph — in order to relive the memory of the occasion.

7. BE THANKFUL: Send a note of appreciation to the host(s).

MAKE YOUR OWN HEADLINE

Which of the above keys can you activate to increase the impact and memories of "power seat" opportunities?

...Martha was distracted by all the preparations that had to be made... [but] "Mary has chosen what is better [sitting and visiting with Jesus]...."
Luke 10:40,42 NIV

A group of tourists visiting New York City needed a van — not for a year but for one afternoon. They desired to deliver Thanksgiving meals and gifts to needy families. The only problem was that on this Thanksgiving weekend all the rental places were out of vans. There appeared to be no way to get one until a member of the group got an idea.

ANTHONY ROBBINS

Anthony Robbins turned to his friends and boldly said, "Look, the bottom line is that if we want something bad enough, we can make it happen! All we have to do is begin to take action. The problem is not that there are no vans in New York City. There are plenty of vans in this city. Look down the street! Look up the street! Do you see all the vans? The only problem is that we just don't have one."

"LET'S GO GET ONE!"

Fresh with that awareness the group determined to get a van. First, they tried walking out in front of vans that were driving down the street.

Although they waived their hands, the drivers not only didn't stop, they sped up.

Then they tried waiting by a traffic light. When a van stopped for a red light one of them would knock on the window. As the driver rolled it down, the group member would say, "Today is Thanksgiving. We'd like to help some needy families. Would you drive us to a certain underprivileged area here in New York City?"

That didn't work either.

Then they tried walking up to stopped vans and offering the drivers $100 to transport them. That got attention, but when the drivers were told where the members wanted to go, they all said, "No."

Robbins' friends were about ready to give up when he exclaimed, "It's the law of averages: sooner or later somebody is going to say yes."

Sure enough, just then the perfect van drove up to the traffic light where the group was standing. It was extra big and could accommodate all of them. When they asked the driver to help them, he said, "I'd be happy to take you," as he reached over and grabbed a hat. When he put it on, they noticed what was written on it: "Salvation Army."

The man drove them to a grocery store, and then they all went out and spent the afternoon blessing people.

This story is a good illustration of leadership in action. Leaders are those people who, when faced with the unexpected challenges that life presents, find a way to overcome shortage or adversity.

Mark Victor Hansen, co-author of *Chicken Soup for the Soul*, believes, "Once you know what you want, the resources of time, money and people will show up."[1]

As Anthony Robbins says, "You can make most anything happen if you commit to it and take action. Miracles like this happen every day — even in a city where 'there are no vans.'"

What shortage or obstacle has been preventing you from a desired outcome? What action can you take to make something happen?

...why stand ye gazing...?
Acts 1:11

Guns, clubs, mace, and handcuffs are the normal weapons used by police. However, this officer lived because he possessed a different type of weapon, a defensive weapon — his vest.

Achievers are people who are masters in the art of taking the offensive and achieving victory. They are goal-oriented, self-motivated individuals who are skilled at overcoming difficulties and fighting through obstacles.

As important as this offensive thinking is, for achievers to enjoy continuing success, they must possess an additional mindset — defensive thinking.

Lou Holtz, former head football coach at Notre Dame, says, "You can't be a great team if you can't play defense."

Real estate tycoon Donald Trump noticed this defensive mindset when he got involved with professional boxing. To his surprise, he observed that "in the end, victory usually goes to the guy who is more difficult to hit. Boxing is really the art of self-defense."

A DEFENSIVE MINDSET

Having a defensive mindset is a Biblical concept. One place it is clearly explained is in Ephesians 6:13-17 NIV, in which the Apostle Paul admonishes us to "put on the full armor of God." He then lists six articles of personal armament: belt, breastplate, foot protectors, shield, helmet, and sword. Note that of the six articles of warfare only one is offensive (the sword). The other five are defensive.

The most talented coaches, generals, and leaders are those who, while maintaining aggressive forward momentum, look for any areas of weakness in their defense. They then "shore up" these areas to protect themselves from unexpected attacks and losses.

This was one of the success secrets of Bill Clinton's presidential campaign. He created a "war room" in which trained staff members would immediately devise replies and defensive strategies to counter any of the opposition's attacks.

If you want to avoid needless wasted time and energy spent handling multitudes of unexpected problems, then bring this defensive thinking into every major area of your life: financial, physical, marital, spiritual, etc.

In life, as in sports, the winning team is not normally the one that scores the most points, but the one that can maintain its lead by keeping the opposition from scoring against it.

To achieve continual success, bring defensive thinking into every major area of your life. Investing time and money in prevention is far better and less stressful than in crisis reaction.

MAKE YOUR OWN HEADLINE

What can you do to increase your defensive awareness?

_____

...put on the full armor...
Ephesians 6:13 NIV

_____

Sins Of Son Cost Parents Court Fines — And Grief

A couple whose teenage son burglarized churches and kept marijuana plants in his bedroom closet was recently found guilty, under the city's Parental Responsibility Ordinance, of failing to control their son.

Some cities are attempting to deal with the negative behavioral problems of underage youths by legally holding parents responsible for the actions of their children. The question is, what is being done about parents who create problems and shame for their kids by their negative actions?

DICK BERNAL

He is pastor of a large church in California. At a recent ministers' conference he shared how the issue of shame, as it pertained to his childhood, had affected his life.

"On the first day of school, my kindergarten teacher asked each child to stand up and tell what their dad did for a living. One by one little boys and girls stood up and proudly proclaimed, 'My daddy does this...my daddy does that...'

"I was sitting in the back of the class. I didn't know my daddy and had no idea what he did. He was a big ole good-looking fellow that about every six months would stop by and try to get my mom in bed, leave a dollar bill for me, and go off again for another six months."

THE FORCE OF SHAME

"I didn't know what to say. The kid sitting right next to me stood up and said, 'My daddy owns a gas station.' The teacher looked at me and said, 'Dicky? Your turn.' I slowly stood up, took a deep breath and I said, 'My daddy owns a gas station too!' and sat down.

"That was the first time in my life I realized I had to carry the shame for the actions of someone. Many of us are born into these situations; others have them placed upon us by the behavior of friends, relatives, or others. The feeling of shame comes when people or society says, 'You don't measure up.'

"That shame was in me. It caused me to feel inferior to others. Throughout my life it caused an occasion to embellish events and sometimes not to totally tell the truth about some situations in order to avoid embarrassment.

"A few months ago, I realized how this negative force had affected my life. I lifted my hands and said, 'God forgive me and get Your fire down inside of me. Kill the things that have brought the plague of shame in my life.'"

The power of God was released afresh in Dick's life that day. The spiritual release that he felt has given him new self-appreciation and confidence in life. He is no longer held captive by the negative memory of a dad who deserted him. Now he has a fresh relationship with a heavenly Father Who will never leave him or forsake him.

The dictionary says that shame is "a loss of regard or honor."[1] It may also be described as a painful feeling of guilt for improper behavior of self or others. If you are suffering from this feeling, do what Dick Bernal did and release the burden to God through prayer.

Are there forces such as shame or negative memories that have hindered you from enjoying life to its fullest? How are you going to overcome them?

[Jesus said] ...your sorrow will be turned to joy.
John 16:20 NASB

Blind Man Robs Bank Then Can't Find Way Out

A man who handed a threatening note to a bank teller and collected $105.00 was apprehended. Police said that the teller realized the man was blind when he asked her to help him leave the building.

At certain times in their lives many people get so bogged down in problems or misery that they seemingly cannot find their way out. Such was the case with...

FLORENCE LITTAUER

Along with her husband, Fred, she conducts marriage seminars and teaches on personality types in church groups, conferences, and conventions nationwide.

Cindy and I have appeared on the same program with Florence and Fred at numerous conferences, and they are always a big hit. Her book, *Personality Plus*, is a classic among those who study personality differences.

The Littauers' own lives took a dramatic change after their two brain-damaged sons died. They found themselves in a desperate search to find their way out of the misery and to find answers to the unanswered questions in their life. They often share the story when they speak.

"Each one of us is different, unique, so that we can function in our roles."
— Florence Littauer

"We were achieving on the surface, but we were hurting underneath," says Florence. "Fred went to the library and started studying books on religion. We came to the realization that our problem was that we needed a spiritual force in control of our lives.

"I learned this principle of control through the experiences with my two brain-damaged sons before they died. Each one had been beautiful to look at — bright blue eyes, blond hair, and dimpled chins. They had eyes, but they could not see; ears, but they could not hear; feet, but they could not walk. They looked all right on the outside, but without a proper functioning brain, with no controlling mechanism, nothing worked.

"We were a lot like those boys. We looked all right on the outside, but inside, nothing much was working right.

"Within a year, each of us, at different times and places, accepted Jesus as our Savior, and gave Him control of our lives."

Fred and Florence not only received a new-found peace and sense of purpose, but as they continued to study the Bible they developed a fresh awareness that not everyone was created by God to function alike. Each person is unique, different.

This understanding of uniqueness helped Florence to launch her career of teaching people to recognize, appreciate, and build successful teams using the personality differences of others.

In reality, how people handle their differences with others will determine their level of success or failure.

Gary Smalley is one of America's premiere teachers in the arena of marital success. His wife states, "Gary and I have seen over and over that one of the major factors that determines whether a marriage succeeds or fails is how the husband and wife handle their differences."[1]

Former NFL Minnesota Vikings coach, Bud Grant, found that learning and merging players' strengths, weaknesses, and differences together into a cohesive unit was one of a head coach's most important jobs. He stated, "As a football coach, you must learn to adapt to your personnel. You have to work with what you have and build a system that fits."[2]

To effectively lead, you must determine that you are not going to let people's differences be an irritation to you, but instead you are going to appreciate them and build upon them.

MAKE YOUR OWN HEADLINE

Do you appreciate individual differences? How can you better use the unique talents and gifts of others in your business or family?

For the body is not one member, but many.
1 Corinthians 12:14

Doorman Refuses To Hail Cab For Hotel Guests

A vacationing couple wanting a taxi reported that a New York City hotel doorman refused to help them get a cab. Instead he told them to take a hike.

The doorman's attitude may sound like the height of rudeness and insensitivity. Actually he was being considerate. When the couple asked for a cab he informed them that it was only one block to their destination and that they could save the cab fare. The couple gave the doorman a good tip and took a nice walk.

Newspaper columnist Dr. Paul Donohue, M.D, says that any kind of exercise is good. However, for most people a good exercise program requires more than occasional leisurely strolls of one block.

DR. KENNETH COOPER

Years ago he began an intensive study of people who exercised. He discovered "notable physical and medical improvements in people who maintained a regular exercise program."

However, he also found that if a person's exercise program was directed only at muscle building, the individual never achieved real physical fitness. In his book *Aerobics* he explains...

How Much Exercise Is Enough?

Dr. Cooper believes that "one of the great misconceptions in the field of exercise is the myth that muscular strength or agility means physical fitness. The muscles that show are just one system in the body, and by no means are the most important.

"The key to fitness is oxygen. In the body the fuel is food, and the flame is oxygen. The body can store food, but it can't store oxygen.

"This is what separates the men from the boys, the fit from the unfit. Most people can produce enough energy (oxygen in their blood) to perform ordinary daily activities. However, if their activities become more vigorous, they can't keep up.

"As one increases his oxygen capability he increases his endurance and overall fitness. This spread — the difference between a person's minimum requirements and his maximum capacity — is the measure of his fitness."[1]

Dr. Cooper believes that he found the secret to effective exercising programs when he identified oxygen consumption as the key measuring device for fitness. He then became famous as he measured needed oxygen consumption of different types of exercises and developed the aerobic exercise program which is used by thousands of people the world over.

Dr. Cooper states that "aerobics is that form of exercise which forces the body to consume increased amounts of oxygen and as such is the only form of exercise that benefits not just the skeletal muscles but the whole body."[2]

He concludes, "There is nothing exotic about any exercise program — but this one works."[3]

In what ways would your productivity and enjoyment of life increase if you were more physically fit? How do you treat your body? How do you expect it to serve you?

Beloved, I wish above all things that thou mayest prosper and be in health, even as thy soul prospereth.

3 John 2

Graham Awarded Congressional Medal

Billy Graham was awarded the Congressional Gold Medal at ceremonies attended by Senators, Congressmen, and the President of the United States.

Cindy and I were privileged to be at that special banquet honoring Reverend Graham for "outstanding and lasting contributions to morality, racial equality, family, philanthropy, and religion."

Billy Graham is the most widely known and respected evangelist in the world today. He has been featured more than 30 times on the annual Gallup poll's "World's Most Admired Men." For more than 50 years he has filled sports stadiums around the world with the simple message that people need spiritual fulfillment in their lives and that it comes by accepting Jesus as Savior.

Even though he is fighting Parkinson's disease that has made it impossible for him to drive or write by hand, Billy is still making the most of his days.

For instance, an estimated 2.5 billion people in 220 countries tuned in during April 1996 to watch the Billy Graham television special, "Starting Over."

When he was a young man, Billy's life changed as a result of something his father did. His dad invited 30 or so local farmers, who were suffering economically from the Depression and despairing for their future, for a day of prayer in his barn.

As a result of this encounter, Billy started attending a local church. Soon thereafter, at a service while the choir sang, Billy responded to the invitation to accept Jesus as his Savior. He describes the experience...

"JUST AS I AM"

"I didn't have any tears or feel any emotion. I didn't hear any thunder or see any lightning, but right there I made my decision for Christ. It was as simple as that...and as conclusive."

Over the next few months, it was obvious to him that "something tremendous" had happened to him on the inside. His school principal noticed, and his mother did also: "Billy was more thoughtful, he had become very kind."

Deep within, though scarcely understood, he sensed a friendship beginning with "Someone" as real as the flesh-and-blood people around him. The whole world seemed different. He had no doubt that he was experiencing what the Bible refers to as the New Birth.

Shortly thereafter, Billy found himself enrolling in Bible school and training for the ministry. During this time, he was asked to "fill in" at a local church meeting taking place at a converted meat market. At the conclusion of his message he gave a salvation appeal. Out of the 100 or so people present, 32 came forward for prayer. Billy Graham's ministry had begun.

One of his secrets of success has been his commitment to have a life and ministry of character. In 1948, he wrote the Modesto Manifesto, which was a behavior policy guide for him and his staff. It included rules such as: "Never be alone with a woman other than your wife" and "Maintain open finances."[1]

Over the years, Billy Graham has called upon more than 100,000,000 people to accept Jesus as their personal Savior. Many of them have responded, not only because of his anointed messages, but because of his exemplary life.

MAKE YOUR OWN HEADLINE

Have you acknowledged Jesus as your Savior? Do people see a "Christian consistency" in your life? If not, in what ways might a relationship with this Higher Power affect your life?

[Jesus answered] "...You must be born again."
John 3:7 NIV

NASA officials employed a "success" strategy that should be considered by all achievers before making major decisions.

I first became aware of this thought process personally at a very earlier age. As a nineteen-year-old newlywed, I needed a summer job between college semesters that would maximize my income. I settled on driving a large delivery truck for a soda pop company in Los Angeles.

One day I had to make a delivery to the back of a store. The only way to get there was to drive down an alley. In order to enter the alley, I had to negotiate a wide turn in the street, using an empty parking place to get a sharp enough angle.

After making the delivery, I started to back up to leave. To my horror, I saw that a car was now parked in that "empty" parking space. I was stuck in the alley until the driver returned and moved the vehicle. At that moment I learned a powerful principle that has guided my life.

Always Have An Exit Strategy!

I have employed this thinking in many areas from learning the location of the nearest emergency exit upon checking into a hotel to leaving maneuvering room between my vehicle and the next car when parallel parking.

I also use it in the business area. Often, before entering into a transaction, I ask myself, "What will be my costs and/or options if this deal doesn't work?"

For example, I make use of it whenever my staff negotiates a contract with a hotel for seminar or convention space. Since we know that we are going to honor our commitment, we always place great emphasis on minimizing the possible penalties if, for some reason, the number of attendees turns out to be lower than expected.

I also use it in hiring new employees. Frequently, we require that they complete a thirty-day trial period so that both parties can determine whether the relationship is a good working arrangement that should continue.

Using exit thinking in business does not imply a sense of untrustworthiness or a lack of commitment. It merely indicates that both parties are considering all possible ending scenarios before entering into a binding agreement.

To protect yourself, before entering into a major contract, I suggest that you do the following:

1. Seek counsel from wise and experienced Christian leaders about the course you are contemplating. Avoiding an unworkable agreement is better than having to develop a strategy for termination of it.

2. Pray and listen to the "inner voice" (not your brain or emotions) for directions concerning the contemplated decision.

3. Consider the need for an exit strategy. What it should be, and how it should be implemented?

There are times when exit strategy thinking is not necessary and may even be counterproductive. However, considering the above points could help you avoid needless future heartaches, personal calamities, lost friendships, and/or vexing legal problems.

MAKE YOUR OWN HEADLINE

How often do you make exit strategy a part of your thinking and negotiating strategy for major decisions? How might such a strategy help you avoid future losses?

There is a way which seemeth right...but the end [is destruction].
Proverbs 14:12

J C Penny To Buy Eckerd Drug Stores

J C Penny moved to expand big time into the drug store business with an agreement to buy Eckerd Drug Stores in a cash-and-stock deal worth about $2.59 billion.

Jack Eckerd, founder of one of the nation's largest drug store chains, built his business around the concept of superior customer service and valuing employees. He recently stated, "If I've learned anything in business it is that your employees are your most important asset."

Eckerd is not alone. Businesses across the nation are coming to a fresh realization that to most customers, their employees create the perceived image of their business and are the key to their continued success.

Sam Walton, founder of Wal-Mart, recognized the value of his workers to his corporate image and company's success. He decided to recognize their importance by not referring to them as "employees" but as "associates."

A Tampa-based bank instituted an attitude and sales training course for all of its employees. It trained them in developing customer relations, maintaining positive and friendly attitudes, and selling additional bank services to customers. The program helped increase bank profits by more than 500 percent in one year.

"For years I covered up the empty space inside me with hard work."
— Jack Eckerd

Jack Eckerd believes that corporate emphasis on the value of people is the prescription for success. However, he struggled to find the right prescription for success in his personal life.

FINDING THE RIGHT PRESCRIPTION

"I knew the retailing game inside out and knew just what it took to be a winner — outwit the competition and get there first with a new idea or product. I learned to be strong, independent, and take charge of situations.

"Building two run-down drug stores in Florida into a chain of 1,700 stores in 15 states left little time for philosophizing about the meaning of life. For years I covered up the empty space inside me with hard work.

"However, several years ago, sensing a need in my life, I started attending a Bible study. I began to mull the claims of Christ over in my mind.

"One day a friend said to me, 'You business people make all these tough decisions about money, but when it comes to something that will affect you for eternity, you keep sitting on the fence. When are you going to make up your mind about Jesus Christ?'"

That statement grabbed Jack Eckerd's attention. Soon thereafter, by accepting Jesus as Savior, he found "The Prescription" to fill his "empty space inside."

MAKE YOUR OWN HEADLINE

Have you discovered your personal "spiritual prescription?" If not, what are you going to do about it? When?

...Believe on the Lord Jesus Christ, and thou shalt be saved....
Acts 16:31

Jet Crashes In Portland

A jet airliner that had circled the Portland airport for nearly an hour because its landing gear wouldn't go down crashed in a field just short of the runway. One hundred and seventy-four passengers miraculously survived.

"Mayday! Mayday! We're going down!" was the urgent message the pilot sent out shortly before the jet crashed. While the crew had been concentrating on solving the landing gear problem, they had failed to realize the severity of another developing problem: the plane was running out of fuel.

This is not an isolated example. According to USA Today, over the last nine years, 39 passenger planes have taken off, or left the gate, without enough fuel.

This is a problem some achievers face. I have personally known many success-oriented people who set their goals and started on their flight to success only to drop out of sight, because they didn't have sufficient "fuel" to finish the course.

During a recent seminar in Little Rock, Arkansas, I was visiting backstage with Tom Hopkins, one of the world's top sales trainers. That day he made a profound statement concerning success: "The single most important ingredient to success is the ability to last."

Shortly thereafter, I was talking with a friend who had just interviewed an elderly man who is one of the world's premiere religious leaders. During the interview my friend asked the minister what, more than anything else, was his secret to achieving. The man replied, "I lasted."

Jesus taught on this concept of having a mindset to finish in the story He told of the ten virgins who went to attend a wedding feast. (Matthew 25:1-13.) All ten women brought their lamps and used them while they were waiting outside for the doors to open and the feast to begin. However, the wait took longer than expected, and the lamps started to go out. Five of them had brought extra oil and refilled their lamps on the spot. The other five had brought no reserves and had to leave to purchase more oil. While they were gone, the doors to the feast were opened. The five who had reserves entered in, while the five who had had to leave missed the celebration.

If you desire to achieve continuing success, it is critical that you have long-term thinking. You must be certain that you have enough energy, resources, and motivation to finish the course.

"THE FUELING EDGE"

There are several things that you can do in the natural arena to stay "fueled up."

- MAKE A "DREAM LIST" AND STAY MOTIVATED. Regularly talk about, see, and touch its items.

- ASSOCIATE WITH SUCCESSFUL PEOPLE. Pick up their attitudes and habits. Learn their success secrets.

- ATTEND POWER-PACKED MEETINGS. Gain knowledge on how to endure and experience breakthroughs.

- LISTEN TO MOTIVATIONAL AND TEACHING TAPES. Repetition is the best way to get new truths imbedded into your subconscious.

- MAKE POSITIVE CONFIRMATIONS. Your world is framed by your words. Talk about your desired destinations.

- READ MIND-BUILDING BOOKS. Learn how to better activate success principles that will empower and motivate you.

- IDENTIFY FUEL LEAKS. Eliminate or reduce those things that drain you of productive energy and creativity.

- SUSTAIN SPIRITUAL STRENGTH. Through regular devotions keep your "spirit man" strong.

Don't run out of fuel short of the destination of your dreams. Keep your tanks topped off by investing time in personal mental, physical, and spiritual renewal.

MAKE YOUR OWN HEADLINE

How can you extend the range of your days? Your life? What are you doing to maintain your "fueling edge" physically? Mentally? Spiritually?

But he [Jesus] said unto them [the disciples], I have meat [fuel] to eat that ye know not of.
John 4:32

Woman Rides Out Tornado In Bathtub

When a tornado ripped through her town, a local woman jumped into her bathtub for safety. As the tornado shattered her house, the fierce winds blew the tub into the woods. She then crawled out to safety.

SUE BOSS

Our friend Sue Boss experienced a different kind of storm one night. More than destroying her home, it ripped through her heart and shattered her life.

"It was like everything I had was gone, in one day. Our church group was returning from attending the passion play in Eureka Springs, Arkansas. My son was on his motorcycle. Following him were my husband and our pastor riding together on his bike.

"Apparently my son, who had been up studying all the night before, fell asleep. His cycle crossed the center line and hit an 18-wheeler truck head on. The impact instantly killed my son. It also caused axle damage to the truck which caused the driver to lose control of his rig. The truck then crossed the center line and struck the second bike, killing my pastor and my husband.

"I was just numb. Most of my family was gone. I didn't know if we had $10 or $10,000, or if we even had life insurance. To make matters worse, there was a good possibility the trucking company was going to sue me."

Sue was able to survive this tragic event, because the power of God undergirded her in her season of grief and gave her comfort and hope. Becoming very active in a local church helped her work through her grief. Some time later, she met a sharp businessman at the church who was a widower. After a season of courtship, they were married.

Today they serve as pastors of a thriving church in Austin, Texas, which has a strong community outreach and buses over 1,000 kids a month to church, proving that there can be a beautiful future even after it appears that dreams are destroyed.

Tom Landry believes that "your reaction to adversity will determine your success or failure as a leader."[1]

Norman Vincent Peale

If you are facing a crisis, the late Dr. Vincent Peale, author of *The Power of Positive Thinking*, gave some great suggestions that can help you.

Five Crisis-Ending Keys

1. Take Charge: God gives each of us the responsibility and the power to take charge of our lives, and to do what needs to be done. Don't let a negative experience of your past be the defining moment of your future. (Acts 27:9,10.)

2. Say Good bye To Fear: In a crisis, the worst thing you can do is give in to fear. Again and again in the Bible God tells people not to fear. (Deuteronomy 1:21; Isaiah 35:4.) Have faith in the future.

3. Do All You Can: When you do your best, God adds His best, and miracles can happen.

4. BE AN ENCOURAGER: Find some activity that helps others. When you encourage others, you fill your own heart with courage.

5. TRUST GOD: If you get mad at God, thinking He is the problem, you have nowhere to go for help. If you quit God, you're finished. God is a restorer. If you turn to Him, you will find yourself supported by a power greater than your problem.[2]

MAKE YOUR OWN HEADLINE

What negative experience or loss have you suffered that may be causing you to think about giving up? If you quit, how many others will suffer by not experiencing the gift of your life?

...though I walk through the valley of the shadow of death, I will fear no evil; for thou art with me....
Psalm 23:4

Ruth Graham's Miracle

She teetered on the brink of death for five days with blazing 104-degree fever brought on by spinal meningitis. Her husband Billy Graham prayed for a miracle. Suddenly, Ruth sat up in bed, asked the nurses for ice cream, and then pleaded to go home.

Prayer helped Ruth Graham to recover quickly. Recent studies have shown that prayer can be a powerful force for healing for others, as well.

A recent study released by the American Academy of Family Physicians found that virtually all doctors surveyed believe in a link between the spirit and the flesh of their patients.[1]

For example, in the first known study linking religious faith and prayer to heart patient recovery, a public hospital in San Francisco took 400 heart patients and divided them into two groups. In the double-blind study, one group was prayed for by strangers who received their names, while the other group was not prayed for. The group that was not prayed for suffered congestive heart failure two and a half times greater than the other group.[2]

In another study conducted in 1995, the Dartmouth medical school tracked 232 open-heart surgery patients for six months. They found that "the patients who received no strength or comfort from religious faith were over three times (300 percent) more likely to die."[3]

CHARLES STANLEY

Charles Stanley, renowned author and pastor of First Baptist Church in Atlanta, says, "For a long time the deity of the Holy Spirit was nothing more to me than Orthodox theology. That is, until I began to think about the fact that (as a Christian) the Holy Spirit dwells in me."[4]

The presence of the Holy Spirit can enable anyone to live a life of greater victory over circumstances.

HOW TO BREAK NATURAL POWER

I gained some fresh insight into this subject as I was studying the story of what happened to Moses at the burning bush. (See Exodus 2,3.)

The Bible says that Moses came to "the mountain of God," and there he found a burning bush. Throughout the Bible, the use of fire often denotes the presence of the Holy Spirit. Therefore, it could be said that when Moses came to the burning bush, he came into the presence of the Holy Spirit.

A particular aspect of this story caught my attention. It was the phrase, "...the bush burned with fire, and the bush was not consumed" (Exodus 3:2). Natural law dictates that bushes on fire burn up. They are consumed. Why wasn't this one?

As I pondered this passage, the revelation that I received has tremendously impacted my life. The only difference that I could find between other bushes and this particular bush that would not be consumed was its location. The Bible says that it was located on "holy ground" (verse 5) — the place of the presence of the Holy Spirit.

Then it hit me: the bush wasn't consumed because when the Holy Spirit is on the scene in great strength, natural laws lose their power.

When Billy Graham prayed for his wife, Ruth, this power released healing into her body. Through prayer, you also have this power available to you. It is the power to overcome adversity, the power to change the course of natural events.

The late Norman Vincent Peale stated that "prayer is a way of increasing our sensitivity to the spiritual aspects of life. From this point of view it is much like exercise in that a person's muscles become responsive by training...."[5]

If you desire to become more effective with prayer, then it is critical to schedule times of personal devotions and worship. By having a strong presence of the Holy Spirit in your life, you will experience unexpected increase and supernatural victories.

MAKE YOUR OWN HEADLINE

How strong a force is the Holy Spirit in your life? What can you do to cause an increase of His presence?

...the bush burned with fire, and the bush was not consumed....
Exodus 3:2

The worst air disaster in aviation history took place as two jets exploded on a runway in dense fog on the Canary Islands.

As a passenger on a Pan-Am jet en route to a vacation cruise in the Mediterranean, this business owner from California had no idea that his life would forever be changed in a few tragic moments.

NORM WILLIAMS

After several hours of flying on a jet across the Atlantic that was then diverted to an alternate airport, Norm Williams and his business associate were anxiously anticipating the short flight to their port city, getting on the cruise ship, and enjoying a time of rest and relaxation.

Their Pan-Am airliner was finally taxing down the single runway at Tenerife airport. Unknown to the passengers, through the dense fog that had engulfed the airport, their terrified pilot saw fast approaching lights on the runway in front of him. Panic gripped him as he realized that it was another plane taking off on the same runway.

The pilot screamed on the radio, "We're on the runway." He then gunned his engines and veered sharply to the left in a desperate maneuver to avoid a crash — but it wasn't far enough or fast enough. The jets collided.

Norm remembers, "There was instant fire, explosions, screams, falling ceilings, and havoc. Searing flames shot through the cabin as explosions blasted through the plane. People who were only inches apart were suddenly separated, one to life and one to death.

"At that moment I cried out, 'In the name of Jesus, through Your shed blood, I stand upon Your Word.'

"I have never sensed the presence of the Holy Spirit as I did then. God imbued me with power from on high. I felt like Superman. I was programmed to survive. Even though I was a part of the tragedy I was separated from fear, insulated from death.

"As I looked for a way of escape I continued to shout, 'Lord, I stand on Your Word.'

"At that moment I looked up. Miraculously, I noticed that there was a gash in the cabin ceiling revealing the sky above, but it would be impossible for me to lift my six-foot, 250-pound frame some ten feet to grab the ragged edges of that blasted fuselage in order to exit.

"How it happened, I will never know — but I did it. I was out and standing on the oily wing from which I jumped 30 feet to the ground below. I hurriedly hobbled away from the burning plane. After going about 100 yards, I heard a loud ground-shaking explosion. I jerked myself around. My plane had disappeared in the flaming inferno."

In the Bible, Shadrach, Meshach, and Abed-nego faced a similar fate as Norm Williams. At the king's order, they were thrown into a fiery furnace. In Daniel 3:27 we read, "...the princes, governors, and captains...saw these men, upon whose bodies the fire had no power...."

Afterwards, the king stated that he believed they were saved from death by God sending an angel to deliver them because they "trusted in him" (v. 28).

Norm believes that his life was spared because, for years he had spent time studying and reading the Bible until its teachings of divine protection had become a part of his inner being. Also, he attributes this miraculous incident to a few moments he and his mom spent together shortly before the flight.

"We both put our hands on the Bible," he recalls, "and prayed for protection and safety."[1]

MAKE YOUR OWN HEADLINE

Are the protection Scriptures of the Bible imbedded in your subconscious so that they will automatically flow out in time of crisis?

"...I will be with thee...when thou walkest through the fire...."
Isaiah 43:2

Man Discovers He Forgot Wife

When a man who was driving from Texas arrived in Oklahoma City he was informed that he had driven off and left his wife at a highway service station.

I have never left my wife behind. However, there was a time when I almost had to fly off and leave my ten-year-old daughter, Michelle, behind at one of the world's busiest airports. However, I believe she experienced a miracle that day because she had learned the power of her spoken words.

There is incredible power in the words that we speak. Biofeedback research now offers amazing evidence that words even affect body functions. In numerous studies, spoken words have been shown to have the ability to lower body temperature, relax muscles, and decrease or increase pulse rate.

Spoken words can also release faith (or fears) that have been stored up on the inside. The Bible even goes so far as to say that literally life and death themselves are in the power of the tongue. (Proverbs 18:21.)

As part of all our children's success-oriented training routine, beginning at the age of eight, they were required to listen to at least one teaching tape each week and turn in a tape report. Therefore, by the time of this event at the airport, Michelle had been listening to motivational and Bible-oriented teaching tapes for more than two years. Because of this exposure, a love for Jesus and the Bible had been implanted in her life. In addition, "possibilitizing" and faith in God had begun to take hold of her thinking, even at this young age.

Therefore, at this moment of personal crisis, in her inner being, faith in God was greater than her fears. I believe that it literally caused her to overcome an impossibility.

"DADDY, I STILL BELIEVE...."

Little Michelle was so looking forward to the trip, having daddy to herself, and being in San Francisco together.

However, when I got to the boarding gate I was faced with a dilemma. The plane was oversold. I had a confirmed advance assigned seat, but the agent said there was no seat for my daughter. I knew that I had to get on the plane because I was obligated to speak that night in Northern California.

I quickly tried checking with other airlines for space, but they were all full. I tried begging with the agent for a seat, to no avail. Fifteen other stand-by passengers, who also had no seats, were standing around the boarding gate trying to get on the plane. There seemed to be no way for Michelle to go.

After several minutes, the ticket agent demanded that I immediately board the flight, or he was going to give my seat to someone else. I got down on my knees to tell Michelle that there was no seat and that Mommy would have to take her home.

Tears rolled down her cheeks as she said, "Daddy, I still believe I'll get on that plane."

I quickly tried to comfort her and preserve her precious faith. Just then the gate agent frantically waved to me. As I rushed over to him, he whispered, "I found one empty seat. Take your daughter on the plane with you."

Little Michelle quickly and happily boarded the plane and nestled contentedly into the only empty seat.

After my speaking engagement, we had a wonderful time together in San Francisco riding the cable cars, going to Fisherman's Wharf, and enjoying the sights.

Pastor-speaker Charles Stanley says that "faith is the Holy Spirit's signal to go into action."[1]

I believe that when little Michelle spoke her faith about getting on the plane, God in his mercy impressed the ticket agent to give her the last remaining seat.

There is tremendous power in the tongue. The Apostle James wrote that even though the tongue is little, it can create great things. (James 3:5.)

I am well aware that with some teachers an overemphasis may have been placed upon what people say and not enough on how they live or why they do what they do.

However, as an achiever it is critical that you realize that great good can be released out of your life by talking positively and by speaking faith-filled words into negative situations. Train yourself to speak words that are uplifting, bless others, and speak of desired dreams and results.

MAKE YOUR OWN HEADLINE

Do the words of your mouth create opportunity and bless others? What can you do to make your words more positive?

Death and life are in the power of the tongue....
Proverbs 18:21

Green Lights On Speed Limit Signs

With the nationwide lifting of federal control on speed limits, many states have increased their speed limits somewhat. But Montana leads the pack. During daylight hours, as long as it is reasonable and proper, Montanans can now drive as fast as they choose.

Since most all states now allow drivers to drive faster, people are increasing their speeds. What was previously considered fast may now be thought of as slow, since others are going faster.

This is true not only on the nation's interstates, but also in the business arena. "Fast," "rapid," "quick-acting," and "speedy" are the current buzz words in the business marketplace.

BE A SPEED FANATIC

"Breakfast on time or it's on us," touts Marriott Hotels, while Hilton Hotels advertises, "Don't check in." At many Hilton properties, guests can bypass the front desk, be immediately escorted to their accommodations, and register in their room as their luggage is being delivered by a bell person.

Federal Express has become a worldwide conglomerate with over 100,000 employees by adhering to the slogan and policy, "When it positively has to get there overnight."

In an effort to capture marketshare with time-conscious achievers, many airlines now offer curbside luggage check in, preassigned seating, and advance issued boarding passes.

Many retail stores now feature such things as one-hour photo developing, 15-minute lunches, 10-minute oil changes, and drive-thru windows.

Consumers have a voracious appetite for time-saving goods and services. Those who tap into this trend will experience growth and increase.

The same is also true on an individual level. Businesses are constantly looking for people who can do a quality job quicker. A lady wrote to me from California telling me how she had been discouraged about her income level. Getting the idea from one of my tape seminar series, she started practicing two hours a day to improve her typing skills. In a short time her typing speed went from forty-five to seventy words per minute. As a result of her increased speed and improved skills, she was promoted to a position paying her double what she had been previously making.

However, there is also a danger here. Even though achievers should have a quick-service mindset in the marketplace, they must be careful not to personally become driven people, wildly racing to and fro. In our fast-paced society we must fight to find times and places for peace, quiet, and a slowed-down pace. Otherwise our personal health, spiritual growth, and/or vital relationships will suffer.

Noted author Richard Exley addresses this issue in his book *The Rhythm of Life.*[1] He states, "Without relaxation, solitude and rest...our lives and our relationships will disintegrate faster than we can repair them."

The real secret then is to balance professional quickness with personal rest, worship, and play.

This delicate balance is probably best expressed by a phrase that I often use in my time management seminars: "Learn to be quick, but not in a hurry."

What ideas can you develop to offer your products and/or services to customers quicker while maintaining personal peace?

But this I say, brethren, the time is short....
1 Corinthians 7:29

Mother Battles To Save Son From Gator's Mouth

A twelve-year-old boy who was snorkeling in a river was bitten on the head by an eleven-foot alligator. Seeing the emergency, the boy's mother reached out and yanked him from the gator's grip. The ensuing struggle broke the child's leg, but saved his life.

In times of emergency, many people somehow receive the ability to do what is seemingly impossible. For you, however, this need not be a one-time occurrence, but a way of life.

"Impossible situations are really only problems for which we have no immediate solution," says Dr. Robert Anthony. "Problems are merely the difference between where you are, and where you can be."[1]

For example, flying was thought impossible by many until the Wright Brothers succeeded in 1903. At one time electric lights, telephones, televisions, microwaves, space travel, and cellular phones would all have been thought impossible, yet they are in common use today.

BILL BRIGHT

Bill is the founder and president of Campus Crusade for Christ International, which has a staff of approximately 7,000 in nearly 100 countries. Over the years, he has had to overcome many impossible situations.

"We are called to live supernatural lives."
— Bill Bright

In his book, *Believing God for the Impossible*, he encourages readers to...

LIVE A SUPERNATURAL LIFE

"We hinder God's working in our lives, not only when we doubt or fear, but also when we are satisfied with mediocrity. God has something better for you than you have ever experienced before.

"As believers in Christ we are called to live supernatural lives, to do impossible deeds. Our lives are joined with the One Who spoke and the worlds were framed, to Whom God has given all authority in heaven and earth. He has come to dwell within us in all of His resurrection power. Now we can claim with the apostle Paul: 'I can do everything God asks me to do with the help of Christ who gives me strength and power.'

"To live a supernatural lifestyle we must begin to think supernatural thoughts, make supernatural plans, pray for supernatural results, and expect God to work supernaturally in our own lives."[2]

MAKE YOUR OWN HEADLINE

Are you satisfied living a life of normality? How can you begin to think supernatural thoughts? What seemingly impossible project can you begin?

...the Spirit of Him who raised Jesus from the dead dwells in you....
Romans 8:11 NAS

Going backwards might be dangerous, but sometimes the ability to reverse direction is a necessary skill to possess. This is as true in life as it is in driving.

Have you ever wished you could reverse time and go back and start a day all over again?

Several years ago actor Bill Murray starred in a movie called *Ground Hog Day*. In this comedy he had to keep re-living a particular day all over again until things came out right.

We may not be able to turn back the hands of time, but there are certain occasions when we can literally relive a day. It happened to me.

A few years ago, I flew from Australia to Hawaii. I left Australia on Sunday evening and arrived in Honolulu on Sunday morning. That's right! Because of the International Date Line, I arrived before I left.

It was exhilarating for me to be able to live that day all over again. However, the excitement of starting Sunday all over again was nothing compared to the ecstasy I experienced when I realized I could start a whole year over again.

NEW YEAR'S RESOLUTIONS

Every January, most achievers take time to list their goals and objectives for the coming year. With a rush of enthusiasm and fresh motivation, they excitedly dream and plan the accomplishments they anticipate in their homes, finances, careers, and health for that year.

For many of them, by the end of February, often this enthusiasm has diminished or has been lost altogether. This is because many of their plans, goals, and projects have become bogged down in the "muddy marsh of inertia." Others appear to be sinking altogether in the "quicksand of discouragement."

START ALL OVER — ANYTIME

If this description sounds familiar to you, don't dismay. You can start fresh again. Why? Because some historians now believe that January first is not really New Year's Day.

As evidence of this theory, any language scholar who is familiar with the Latin origins of words is aware that the root names of many months do not correspond to their placement on the calendar.

For instance: The root word for our tenth month, October, actually means eight. The root for our eleventh month actually stands for nine. *Deca*, from which December comes, is interpreted as ten.

Following this logic, January would be the eleventh month and February the twelfth month. That would mean that March first could be New Year's Day.

If that doesn't excite you, consider something else. The federal government operates on what is called a "fiscal year." For purposes of accounting, the New Year begins on July first.

Not only that, but the Internal Revenue Service allows most corporations to pick the first day of any month as the beginning of their "fiscal year." For these companies, New Years Day is the first day of whatever month they choose.

If the historians, the federal government, and corporations can choose to celebrate different New Years Days, so can you.

If you are disappointed with how this year is going so far, don't despair. Analyze where you have failed in the past and what changes you need to make to assure success in the future. Reset your goals. Now, just declare today as your new personal New Years Day. Start the year all over again. Imagine beginning today as you have never done before. Bring a fresh wave of motivation and excitement into your life. Add new thrust to your dreams.

Robert Schuller says, "You can never win if you don't start." So, make today the first day of a brand new future.

Happy New Year!

MAKE YOUR OWN HEADLINE

How would it affect you if you could start the year all over again?

...this one thing I do, forgetting these things which are behind...I press toward the mark....
Philippians 3:13,14

According to the Red Cross, with his last donation of blood, an area man will have given 240 pints, or 30 gallons, of blood during his lifetime.

Bernie Williams is just an ordinary man, a former Marine who fought during World War II. Wanting to do something to help his fellow man, in 1951 he came up with the idea of donating his blood. He has been doing it ever since.

Bernie says, "Not being rich or born with a golden spoon, I had to give what I could. What more could someone do than to help give life to another person?"

I salute Bernie for his compassion and commitment to helping others. He has the right priorities and is doing positive things with his life.

To me, this is an example of what Christianity should be about: reaching beyond our own world to be a blessing.

However, what if someone had the same value system and compassion as Bernie but was also financially successful? Look at how much he could accomplish. What if he were like Bill Gates, who has already donated $270 million to charities? What kind of impact could his life have on others?

This perspective would give your life a purpose. Having a purpose would furnish you with the inner power that would direct and propel your life. The height of your accomplishments will never rise above your level of purpose for living and your dreams. And what greater purpose can you possess than to be a blessing to those in need?

In order to be this kind of person you must be willing to re-define success and measure your life, not by what you get and/or accumulate, but rather by the impact your life can have on others.

Psychologist William James stated, "The only truly happy people I know are those who have found a cause greater than themselves to live for."[1]

I have made this decision and some of my closest friends such as Peter Lowe, Tim Flynn, Don Ostrom, and many others have also. We are immensely successful, but annually release hundreds of thousands of dollars to help others. I don't share this boastfully, but only to paint an image of achieving Christians who care.

If you desire to be a Bernie Williams giving blood, I admire you, and God will bless you. Throughout the Bible God brought increase to those who were willing to release what they had.

However, like many who read this book, you may have determined to achieve great success. If that is so, then why not achieve with a life of giving and significance? Whether you are a Peter Lowe supporting Billy Graham and other ministries, or a Tim Flynn giving away television equipment, or a Don Ostrom supporting missionaries and Bible schools around the world, or a Bob Harrison raising money for Feed the Hungry, you can make a difference in the lives of others. It all begins with a decision — a decision to live beyond self and be a blessing to others.

Create your own "power points." Let them be the places where you have released blessings and God's power into other people's lives. In the words of Bill Gates, "The dream is not about getting rich but about making a difference."[2]

MAKE YOUR OWN HEADLINE

What do you have now that you can give to bless others? What actions can you take this week toward a life of greater significance?

"...Insomuch as ye have done it unto one of the least of these my brethren, ye have done it unto me."
Matthew 25:40

Endnotes

Chapter 1: Turtle
[1]Richard Exley, *The Rhythm of Life* (Tulsa: Honor Books, 1987), p. 28.
[2]Gordon MacDonald, *Ordering Your Private World* (Nashville: Oliver Nelson, 1985), p. 30.
[3]Denis Waitley, *Timing Is Everything* (Nashville: Thomas Nelson Publishers, 1992), pp. 6,7.

Chapter 5: Granny
[1]Robert Schuller, *Power Thoughts* (New York: Harper-Collins Publishers, 1995), p. 92.

Chapter 6: Phantom
[1]Anthony Robbins, *Unlimited Power* (New York: Fawcett Columbine, 1986), pp. 230,231.

Chapter 7: Rich
[1]Dr. Patrick Quillin, *Healing Secrets from the Bible* (Canton: The Leader Company, 1995), p. 21.
[2]Catherine Marshall, *To Live Again* (New York: Fawcett World Library, 1970), p. 42.
[3]Ibid.

Chapter 9: Heart Attacks
[1]Dr. Patrick Quillin, *Healing Secrets From the Bible* (Canton: The Leader Company, 1995), p. 1.
[2]Ibid., p. 7.
[3]Ibid., pp. 53-59.

Chapter 11: Pilot
[1]Dexter Yager, *Don't Let Anybody Steal Your Dream* (Charlotte: Internet Services, 1993), p. 9.
[2]Ibid.

Chapter 13: FDR
[1]Ken Kerr, "Ten Most Common Marketing Mistakes," *Hawaii Christian Leaders Event Highlights*, Harrison International Seminars, Tulsa, 1995.
[2]Joe Girard, *How To Sell Yourself* (New York: Warner Books, 1979), p. 31.

[3]Harvey Mackay, *Beware the Naked Man Who Offers You His Shirt* (New York: Ivy Books, 1990), pp. 226,227.

[4]Edwin Louis Cole, *Maximized Manhood* (Pittsburg: Whitaker House, 1982), p. 127.

Chapter 14: Tear

[1]Dr. James Dobson, *Straight Talk* (Dallas: Word Publishing, 1991), p. 132.

Chapter 15: Circus

[1]Lee Iacocca, *Iacocca — An Autobiography* (New York: Bantam Books, 1984), p. 281.

[2]Bill Gates, "Technology," *Price-Costco Connection*, December 1996, p. 43.

Chapter 16: Fish

[1]Les Brown, *Live Your Dreams* (New York: William Morrow and Company, 1992), p. 49.

Chapter 18: Lightning

[1]Zig Ziglar, *Top Performance* (New York: Berkley Books, 1987), p. 43.

[2]Tom Peters, "Management Excellence," *The Business Journal*, September 9, 1991, p. 24.

[3]Norman Vincent Peale, *Bible Power for Successful Living* (New York: Peale Center for Christian Living, 1993), p. 130.

Chapter 20: Kids Sue

[1]T.D. Jakes, *Loose That Man and Let Him Go* (Tulsa: Albury Press, 1995), pp. 99,107.

[2]Dr. James Dobson, *Straight Talk* (Dallas: Word Publishing, 1991), p. 62.

[3]*God's Little Devotional Book for Dads* (Tulsa: Honor Books, 1995), p. 219.

[4]Lee Iacocca, *Talking Straight* (New York: Bantam Books, 1988), p. 23.

Chapter 21: Beware

[1]Tim LaHaye, *Anger Is a Choice* (Grand Rapids: Zondervan, 1982), p. 156.

[2]Pat Riley, *The Winner Within* (New York: G.P. Putnam's Sons, 1993), p. 175.

Chapter 22: Cadillac

[1]Dr. Joyce Brothers, *The Successful Woman* (New York: Simon & Schuster, 1988), p. 49.

[2]Ibid.

[3]Harvey Mackay, *Beware the Naked Man Who Offers You His Shirt* (New York: Ivy Books, 1990), p. 78.

Chapter 23: Docs
[1]Bill McCartney, *From Ashes to Glory* (Nashville: Thomas Nelson Publishers, 1995), pp. 10,291.

Chapter 24: Coma
[1]Dr. Maxwell Maltz, *Pscyhocybernetics* (New York: Pocket Books, 1960), p. 2.

Chapter 25: Squeeze
[1]Jess Gibson, *Coaching Champions* (Green Forrest, AR: New Leaf Press, 1993), pp. 76,77.

Chapter 26: Shampoo
[1]Charles Stanley, *The Wonderful Spirit-Filled Life* (Nashville: Thomas Nelson Publishers, 1992), p. 4.

Chapter 28: New Bills
[1]Bill Ellis, "Security," *Automotive Age*, date unknown, p. 22.

Chapter 29: Difference
[1]Dexter Yager, *The Mark of a Millionaire* (Charlotte: Internet Services, 1992), pp. 22,23.

Chapter 30: Rats and Roaches
[1]Robert H. Schuller, *Self-Esteem: The New Reformation* (Waco: Word Books, 1982), p. 61.
[2]Zig Ziglar, *Top Performance* (New York: Berkley Books, 1986), p. 91.
[3]Peter Daniels, *Miss Phillips, You Were Wrong* (Plymouth, South Australia: The House of Tabor, 1989), pp. 11-13.

Chapter 31: Governor
[1]Richard Capen, Jr., *Finish Strong* (San Francisco: Harper/Zondervan, 1996), p. 81.
[2]Zig Ziglar, *Top Performance* (New York: Berkley Books, 1986), p. 178.

Chapter 32: Swamp
[1]Edna Harrison-Harlin, *A Second Chance at Love* (Garden Grove, CA: New Lease Publishers, 1984), p. 60.

[2]Ibid., p. 59.

[3]Pat Riley, *The Winner Within* (New York,: G.P. Putnam's Sons, 1993), p. 36.

Chapter 34: Powell

[1]Donald J. Trump, with Tony Schwartz, *Trump: The Art of the Deal* (New York: Warner Books, 1987), pp. 51,52.

[2]Porter B. Williamson, *Gen. Patton's Principles for Life and Leadership* (Tucson: Management & Systems Consultants, 1988), p. 207.

Chapter 35: Princess

[1]Gavin and Patti MacLeod, *Back on Course* (Old Tappan, NJ: Fleming H. Revel, 1981), pp. 181-183.

Chapter 37: Rut

[1]Bill Swad, Sr., *You Can Do It, Too!* (Gahanna, OH: Christian Center, 1991), p. 7.

[2]"Maybe a C?" *New Man* magazine, Lake Mary, Florida, Strang Communications, September 1996, p. 15.

Chapter 38: Bigger

[1]Robert Crandall, "American Sells DC10s," *Financial World*, June 1991.

Chapter 39: Dallas

[1]Tom Landry, *An Autobiography — Tom Landry* (New York: Harper-Collins, 1990), p. 282.

[2]Ibid., p. 279.

Chapter 40: Medium

[1]Lee Iacocca, *Iacocca — An Autobiography* (New York: Bantam Books, 1994), p. 59

[2]Joe Griffith, *Speaker's Library of Business* (Englewood Cliffs, NJ: Prentice Hall, 1990), p. 328.

[3]John L. Mason, *An Enemy Called Average* (Tulsa: Harrison House, 1990), back cover.

[4]These excerpts were taken by permission from: John Mason, *An Enemy Called Average* (Tulsa: Harrison House, 1990); John Mason, *You're Born an Original* (Tulsa: Honor Books, 1993); and John Mason, "Rising Above Average," *Hawaii Christian Leaders Event Highlights*, Harrison International Seminars, Tulsa, 1995.

Chapter 42: Snake
[1]Dr. Maxwell Maltz, *Psychocybernetics* (New York: Pocket Books, 1960), p. 2.
[2]Zig Ziglar, *Top Performance* (New York: Berkley Books, 1987), p. 108.

Chapter 43: Dead Woman
[1]Richard Capen, Jr. *Finish Strong* (San Francisco: Harper/Zondervan, 1996), p. 123.
[2]Jan Stoop and Betty Southward, *The Grandmother Book* (Nashville: Thomas Nelson, Inc., 1993), p. 135.
[3]Arvella Schuller, *The Positive Family* (Garden City, NJ: Doubleday-Galilee, 1982), p. 21.

Chapter 45: Penske
[1]Ray Didinger, *Game Plans* (Boston: Little, Brown, and Company, 1995), p. 39.
[2]Norman Vincent Peale, *Bible Power for Successful Living* (New York: Peale Center for Christian Living, 1993), p. 40.

Chapter 46: Deathbed
[1]Richard Capen, Jr., *Finish Strong* (San Francisco: Harper/Zondervan, 1996), p. 123.

Chapter 48: Blob
[1]*New Webster's Dictionary*, Giant Print Edition, s.v. "depression."
[2]Cheryl Salem, *A Royal Child* (Tulsa: Harrison House, 1995), p. 82.
[3]Ibid., p. 83.

Chapter 49: Driver
[1]*God's Little Devotional Book* (Tulsa: Honor Books, 1995), p. 129.

Chapter 51: Hawaii
[1]Pat Riley, *The Winner Within* (New York: G.P. Putnam's Sons, 1993), p. 165.
[2]Demos Shakarian, *The Happiest People on Earth* (Old Tappan, NJ: Chosen Books, 1975), p. 145.
[3]Patrick Klingaman, *Thank God It's Monday* (Wheaton: Victor Books, 1996), p. 26.

Chapter 53: Bomb
[1]Richard Exley, *The Rhythm of Life* (Tulsa: Honor Books, 1987), p. 60.

[2]Laurie Beth Jones, *Jesus-Led* (New York: Hyperion, 1996), p. 22.

[3]T.D. Jakes, *Loose That Man and Let Him Go* (Tulsa: Albury Press, 1995), p. 93.

Chapter 54: Disappears

[1]Stephen R. Covey, *The Seven Habits of Highly Effective People* (New York: Simon & Schuster, 1989), p. 97.

Chapter 55: Right To Work

[1]Peggy Anderson, *Great Quotes From Great Leaders* (Lombard, IL: Celebrating Excellence Publishers, 1990), p. 76.

[2]Lester Sumrall, *Courage to Conquer* (Tulsa: Harrison House, 1992), p. 138.

[3]Ibid., p. 46.

Chapter 56: Jobs Act

[1]Harvey Mackay, *Beware the Naked Man Who Offers You His Shirt* (New York: Ivy Books, 1990), p. 121.

[2]Ibid.

[3]Joe Griffith, *Speaker's Library of Business Stories* (Englewood Cliffs, NJ: Prentice Hall, 1990), p. 29.

[4]Tom Peters, *Thriving on Chaos* (New York: Harper Perennial Publishing, 1993), p. 90.

[5]Joe Griffith, op. Cit., p. 97.

Chapter 57: Slavery

[1]*The New Horizon Ladder Dictionary*, s.v. "courage."

[2]Quoted in Wynn Davis, *The Best of Success* (Lombard, IL: Great Quotations Publishing Company, 1994), p. 67.

[3]Edwin Louis Cole, *Courage* (Tulsa: Honor Books, 1985), pp. 28,29.

[4]Rosa Parks, *Rosa Parks: The Quiet Strength, Faith, Hope and Heart of a Woman Who Changed a Nation* (Grand Rapids, MI: Zondervan, 1994).

[5]Harvey Mackay, *Beware the Naked Man Who Offers You His Shirt* (New York: Ivy Books, 1990), p. 67.

Chapter 58: Love Field

[1]Zig Ziglar, *Top Performance* (New York: Berkley Books, 1986), pp. 110,111.

[2]Dale Carnegie, *How to Win Friends and Influence People* (New York:

Pocket Books, 1936), p. 57.

Chapter 59: Mines
¹John R. Noe, *Peak Performance Principles for High Achievers* (New York: Frederick Fell Publishers, 1984), p. 96.

Chapter 60: Trapped
¹George Shinn, *Miracle of Motivation* (Wheaton: Living Books, 1981), p. 168.
²Ibid., pp. 169-172.

Chapter 63: Romeo
¹Jim Guinn, "Christian Con Men," *The New Breed*, RMAI, Tulsa, Oklahoma, Fall/Winter 1995.

Chapter 64: Mini-Bars
¹*Travel Weekly*, Reed Publishing, Secaucus, New Jersey, June 1995, p. 12.
²Joe Griffith, *Speaker's Library of Business* (Englewood Cliffs, NJ: Prentice Hall, 1990), p. 319.

Chapter 65: Vultures
¹Pat Boone, *A New Song* (Carol Stream, IL: Creation House, 1970), p. 163.

Chapter 66: Bugs
¹*Business Travel News*, Skokie, Illinois, June 1995.

Chapter 67: Flood
¹Stephen R. Covey, *The Seven Habits of Highly Effective People* (New York: Simon & Schuster, 1989), p. 219.

Chapter 68: Mad Bees
¹Joe Gibbs, *Game Plans for Success* (Boston: Little, Brown and Company, 1995), p. 27.
²Tom Hopkins, *How To Master the Art of Selling* (Scottsdale: Tom Hopkins International, 1982), p. 17.
³Ray Didinger, *Game Plans for Success* (Boston: Little, Brown and Company, 1995), p. 155.
⁴Joe Griffith, *Speaker's Library of Business Stories* (Englewood Cliffs, NJ: Prentice Hall, 1990), pp. 266,267.
⁵Ibid.
⁶Ibid.

Chapter 69: School

[1]Richard Capen, Jr., *Power Points* (San Francisco: Harper/Zondervan, 1996), p. 123.

[2]Dr. Edwin Louis Cole, "Communication and Money," *Hawaii Christian Leaders Event Highlights*, Harrison International Seminars, Tulsa, 1995.

[3]Ibid.

[4]John C. Maxwell, *The Leader Within You* (Nashville: Thomas Nelson Publishers, 1993), p. 97.

[5]Dexter Yager, *Don't Let Anybody Steal Your Dream* (Charlotte: Internet Services, 1993), p. 31.

Chapter 70: Fire

[1]S. Truett Cathy, *It Is Easier To Succeed Than to Fail* (Nashville: Thomas Nelson Publishers, 1989), p. 101.

[2]Ibid.

[3]Ibid., pp. 13,14.

[4]Ibid., p. 16.

Chapter 71: Can

[1]Les Brown, *Live Your Dreams* (New York: William Morrow and Company, 1992), p. 211.

Chapter 79: Blackout

[1]Dennis Byrd, *Rise and Walk: The Trials and Triumph of Dennis Byrd* (New York: Harper-Collins, 1993).

Chapter 81: Snails

[1]Denis Waitley, *Timing Is Everything* (Nashville: Thomas Nelson Publishers, 1992), pp. 130,131.

Chapter 85: Van

[1]Jack Canfield and Mark Victor Hansen, *Dare to Win* (New York: Berkley Books, 1994), p. 35.

Chapter 87: Sins of Son

[1]*The New Horizon Ladder Dictionary*, s.v. "shame."

Chapter 88: Blind Man

[1]Denalyn Lucado, *Promises Promises* (Gresham, OR: Vision House, 1996), p. 38.

[2]Ray Didinger, *Game Plans for Success* (Boston: Little, Brown and

Company, 1995), p. 128.

Chapter 89: Doorman

[1]Kenneth W. Cooper, M.D., *Aerobics* (New York: M. Evans and Company, 1968), pp. 24-26.

[2]Ibid., inside cover.

[3]Ibid.

Chapter 90:Graham

[1]*Los Angeles Times*, November 15, 1993.

Chapter 94: Tornado

[1]Tom Landry, *An Autobiography — Tom Landry* (New York: Harper Paperbacks, 1990), p. 286.

[2]Norman Vincent Peale, *Bible Power for Successful Living* (New York: Peale Center for Christian Living, 1993), pp. 130-133.

Chapter 95: Ruth Graham

[1]Dana Sterling, "Praying to Get Well," *Tulsa World*, Tulsa, Oklahoma, December 19, 1996, pp. A1,A2.

[2]Ibid.

[3]Ibid.

[4]Charles Stanley, *The Wonderful Spirit-Filled Life* (Nashville: Thomas Nelson Publishers, 1992), p. 5.

[5]Norman Vincent Peale, *A Treasury of Courage and Confidence* (New York: Peale Center for Christian Living, 1970), p. 34.

Chapter 96: Collide

[1]Norman Williams, *Terror at Tenerife* (Van Nuys, CA: Bible Voices, Inc., 1977), pp. 19,21,63-65.

Chapter 97: Forgot Wife

[1]Charles Stanley, *The Wonderful Spirit-Filled Life* (Nashville: Thomas Nelson Publishers, 1995), p. 77.

Chapter 98: Speed Limit

[1]Richard Exley, *The Rhythm of Life* (Tulsa: Honor Books, 1987).

Chapter 99: Gator

[1]Dr. Robert Anthony, *How To Make the Impossible Possible* (New York: Berkley Books, 1996).

[2]Bill Bright, *Believing God for the Impossible* (San Bernardino: Here's Life Publishers, 1979), pp. 42,46.

Chapter 101: Blood

[1]Richard Exley, *The Rhythm of Life* (Tulsa: Honor Books, 1987), p. 108.

[2]Bill Gates, "Technology," *Price-Costco Connection*, December 1996, p. 43.

Tape Seminar Series

by Bob Harrison

Creating Financial Increase
Strategies for Success
Wealth and Success
How To Break Free From Debt
Secrets to Financial Turnarounds
Spiritual Warfare and Your Money
Keep Your Money From Going Down the Tube
Effective Time Increase
Winning in Sales
One-Day Turnarounds
Save a Bundle
How To Fly and Stay Free
Better Homes and Marriages
Ever Increasing Love
Your Marriage Matters
You Were Meant To Be Together
Raising Champion Children
Men of Victory
Call — Claim — Command

ABOUT THE AUTHOR

Bob Harrison is recognized as an international authority of success because of his ability to ignite hope in others. He is known world-wide as Doctor Increase, challenging people to overcome seemingly impossible circumstances by inspiring them with practical, down-to-earth strategies and hard-won wisdom.

He speaks from the heart of a man who has lived the gamut of experiences, inspired challenges, near failures, thrilling victories, and astonishing miracles. At one time, he was millions of dollars in debt and on the verge of bankruptcy. He applied his biblical understanding, academic training, and business acumen and released a powerful and dramatic breakthrough in his life.

Bob is a man who cares about people and it shows. The wide range of experience he holds as a sales achiever, business owner, television personality, successful author, and dynamic speaker, has placed him in tremendous demand.

His message has been shared with literally thousands of businesses, corporations, seminar groups, and television audiences world-wide. He specializes in teaching on the healing of marriages and finances, the creative force of increase thinking, and breaking free from the bondage of debt. Countless homes and businesses have been transformed and turned around by applying the principles he shares.

Bob is a Business Management Graduate of California State University. He married his childhood sweetheart, Cindy, and their five children all work with them in their various enterprises. Bob is founder and president of Christian Business Leaders International and Harrison International Seminars, both based in Tulsa, Oklahoma.

For additional information on seminars, scheduling speaking engagements, or to write the author, please address your correspondence to:

P.O. Box 701890
Tulsa, Oklahoma 74170-9926

Or, call: 1-800-632-4653

Tulsa, Oklahoma